W9-BQS-121

# SHARK BITES

## TRUE TALES OF SURVIVAL

### GREG AMBROSE

THE
BESS
PRESS

P. O. Box 22388
Honolulu, Hawai'i 96823

Cover design and illustrations: Kevin Hand

Maps: Bryant Fukutomi

Library of Congress Cataloging-in-Publication Data

Ambrose, Greg.
          Shark bites : true stories of survival /
Greg Ambrose.
                    p.        cm.
          Includes illustrations.
          ISBN 1-57306-054-2
          1. Shark attacks. 2. Sharks.
I. Title.
QL638.93.A42 1996        597.312-dc20

Copyright © 1996 by The Bess Press, Inc.

ALL RIGHTS RESERVED
No part of this book may be reproduced or transmitted in any form by any
means, electronic or mechanical, including photocopying and recording, or by
any information storage or retrieval system, without permission in writing from
the copyright holder.

Printed in the United States of America

First printing, November 1996

## Aloha

This book is dedicated to everyone who loves the ocean and the animals that call it home, but especially to Norene Elena, Lindsey Carissa, Craig, Jeremy and Tina. May all your sharks be friendly.

## Mahalo

*Shark Bites* could never have been written without the help of some very special people. *Mahalo nui loa* to the courageous men and women who confronted the terrible twin demons of fear and death and lived to tell us their tales so that we might be inspired. *Mahalo* to the many authors and experts whose articles and books gave me a better understanding of the most misunderstood animals on the planet; to Kevin and Bryant for their fabulous illustrations and maps; to Revé, Buddy, Ann, Carol and the rest of the Bess Press crew for their hard work; to Norene for her wisdom and adroit editing; and especially to all the shark researchers who toil in frequently dangerous circumstances for paltry monetary compensation to reveal the truth about these magnificent creatures and find ways to keep humans and sharks from interacting to each other's detriment.

## Also by Greg Ambrose:

*Surfer's Guide to Hawaii: Hawaii Gets All the Breaks*

with Sandra Kimberley Hall

*Memories of Duke: The Legend Comes to Life*

# Table of Contents

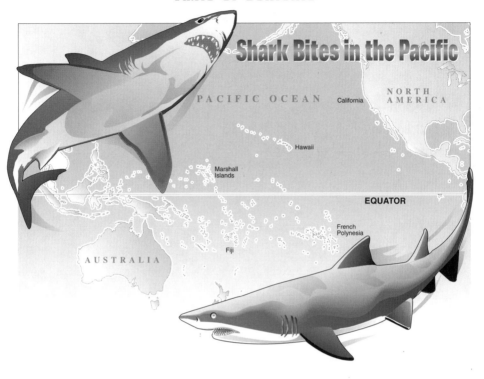

# Introduction

Pity the poor predator.

Sharks developed into the ocean's most efficient hunters over 325 million years of evolution, earning them the loathing of the planet's dominant life form. Rather than admire sharks for their strength, speed and the incredible powers of perception that allow them to cull unfit and ailing animals from the gene pool, humans have come to regard sharks as demons, the devil's own attack dogs, mindless eating machines that prowl the ocean poised to ferociously attack the instant a person dips a toe in the water.

In fact, the reverse is true. Sharks kill about ten humans a year worldwide, while fishermen slaughter at least one hundred million sharks annually. Many are caught incidentally in nets and are tossed overboard to rot, while others are sought for their meat. Costa Rica fishermen alone haul two hundred thousand sharks a year from the ocean to grind their cartilage for an alleged cancer cure that has no scientific validation.

When mainland China reopened trade with the West in 1986, an instant market for shark fins was created to satisfy the insatiable Asian appetite for shark fin soup. Hundreds of thousands of captured sharks are cruelly dumped back into the ocean after their fins are hacked off. Unable to maneuver, they blunder about helplessly and die slowly and terribly of starvation. Which is the more savage species, humans or sharks?

The amazing people who tell their stories in this book were selected because they were attacked while enjoying the most popular things people do in near-shore waters, showing that sharks don't single out any group of ocean users. You can be mauled no matter what fun activity lures you into the ocean. But consider how many millions of people venture into the sea every day, and how few are ever attacked by sharks.

You only have to rub two brain cells together to realize that if sharks awarded humans favored-prey status, there would be hundreds of thousands of fatalities a year worldwide. To survive, an apex predator needs to expend as little energy as possible while capturing a meal, and nothing is as easy to catch in the ocean as humans. We swim slowly, can't breathe underwater, and have no fangs, claws, fur or spikes to protect us. We're like floating Spam without the can, and should be a valuable source of protein for sharks.

But sharks began developing their diet long before the first dinosaurs showed up, while humans have been splashing in the ocean for only a small fraction of that time. We just aren't on the menu, and sharks still treat humans cautiously, as an oddity rather than a meal.

In our short but rapid climb to the throne of the animal kingdom, humans have developed the incredible conceit that we are somehow removed from nature, that we occupy a godlike status above animals and that we control natural forces.

We howl with arrogant outrage when a shark dares to attack a human, forgetting that when we enter the ocean, we shed our mantle of superiority and become just another link in the food chain, and a lowly, vulnerable link at that.

To their credit, Polynesians, Micronesians, Melanesians and people of other cultures with a long tradition of using the ocean for food and frolic haven't demonized sharks the way Westerners have.

Many islanders regard sharks as gods and honor them with special rituals. At worst, they consider sharks merely as competitors in the quest to gather sea life. They think of sharks as among the most graceful and beautiful animals in the ocean, tempering their admiration for their devastatingly efficient hunting skills with a healthy respect for their strength.

It's difficult for some cultures to feel affection toward a creature whose young devour each other in the womb, but fisherman and marine park curator Steve Kaiser has learned to love tiger sharks, among the most feared sharks in the world. Kaiser has a splendid large female tiger shark swimming freely in his aquarium in the Bahamas and walks fearlessly in the water with this dreaded carnivore. People are amazed to see him affectionately pet this predator as he tries to show visitors that tigers aren't the nasty, mean, ugly, snarling animal that everybody thinks they are. "They are kind, gentle creatures," Kaiser says, calling them mellow when compared with other sharks kept in captivity.

If we can overcome our cultural conditioning, we find there is much about sharks to admire, such as their sleek, streamlined hydrodynamic shape, which allows them to speed through a medium eight hundred times more dense than air.

They are splendid models of evolutionary efficiency, superbly suited for a life of active predation. A muscular yet flexible body provides astonishing speed and agility, with lightning turns and blinding acceleration. Sharks can cruise slowly on patrol with a minimum of effort, and with a flick of a powerful tail launch into rapid pursuit.

Sharks are an important part of the ocean ecosystem, weeding out the sick, weak and slow animals to maintain the health of the populations and ensure that no group of animals increases to the detriment of other groups.

The slaughter of the ocean's apex predator could throw the underwater ecosystem out of balance, which could be disastrous for commercial fisheries and the general health of the ocean. As the top ocean hunter, sharks grow slowly, mature late in life and produce few offspring, which makes them especially vulnerable to overfishing. When sharks are killed more quickly than they can reproduce, the population takes decades to recover after crashes from overfishing.

Recognizing that the ocean's greatest hunter is in danger of being wiped out by the planet's most deadly predator, man, some countries have passed laws to restrict or ban the hunting of sharks. The U.S. government in 1993 protected thirty-nine shark species from Maine to Texas that were in danger of being overfished. And South Africa, Australia and California have passed laws safeguarding the world's most magnificent and feared shark, the great white.

Researchers have learned that sharks aren't mindless eating machines, but sophisticated and remarkably intelligent animals. Ironically, these fierce creatures are fragile, difficult to capture, transport and keep alive in captivity. Scientists are desperate to find out precisely how overfishing has devastated shark populations, but these shy and often solitary creatures are extremely difficult to study.

We fear what we do not understand, and sharks have been marvelously effective in eluding all attempts to quantify them. Unlike big cats, bears and other land-based predators, sharks leave no mark as they range far and wide through their trackless wilderness. Some of the more interesting species are extremely dangerous animals that vanish into the mysterious depths with a few swishes of their tail, confounding frustrated researchers.

Some say the great white shark population off California is increasing ever since its favorite prey, seals and sea lions, have been protected from hunting. Others swear that they are in danger of being overfished to extinction, but no one knows for sure.

Scientists lack knowledge of even the most basic facts about sharks, such as how many there are, their mating behavior, reproductive habits, migratory patterns and range, and especially the big question: why they attack humans.

Data is sparse, but theories abound, the favorite being the case of mistaken identity. When a great white shark lurking below spots a diver or surfer near the surface, it perceives the silhouette as a seal and torpedoes its target, launching it into the air with the ferocity of its attack. But when it doesn't taste the expected calorie-rich blubber, it swims away, a good inducement for ocean lovers to diet.

A competing attempt to explain why great white sharks seldom consume the humans they attack is the cautious predator theory. The claws of a frantically struggling seal or sea lion could gouge the eyes of an attacking great white, dooming it to a slow death by starvation. So the shark blasts its prey with a devastating hit, then swims a safe distance away and waits for the creature to bleed to death before returning to leisurely finish its meal. Imagine its surprise when humans don't hang around for the shark to return and devour them.

Marine biologists in Hawai'i were puzzled in 1991 when tiger sharks began attacking humans in unprecedented numbers. It had been thirty years since the last fatal attack, and by 1995 tiger sharks had killed two people, were suspected of killing a bodyboarder whose corpse was never recovered, and had bitten a dozen more people.

Theories were put forth and energetically debated, the favorite being the case of mistaken identity. The endangered green sea turtle had made a dramatic recovery under federal protection, while other favorite prey of tiger sharks were being fished out. One theory had tiger sharks moving closer to shore to feed on the green sea turtles, which put the sharks in the same areas as surfers, swimmers and divers. In water offering poor visibility, the tiger sharks were biting humans and swimming away when they realized they didn't taste or act like their normal prey.

Another explanation was the curious critter theory. Lacking hands, sharks investigate things in their watery world with their mouth, taste testing to find a good meal. And the humans either fight or flee, sending the sharks in the opposite direction.

The scientists realized that these are only theories, and that they knew almost nothing about tiger sharks. Most of what passed as knowledge about tiger sharks was merely folk wisdom, and as researchers began tracking tigers with radio transmitters and tags, they discovered that most of the folk wisdom was actually folk foolishness.

The State of Hawai'i paid lip-service to concern about the tiger shark attacks and funded $20,000 for tracking studies. But as soon as the attacks diminished, the state yanked the money back before the researchers saw a penny of it.

It is becoming increasingly difficult to obtain federal funding for shark research, and if scientists are going to solve the mysteries of where sharks range and how they hunt, the private sector will have to pay to help find methods to keep humans and sharks apart.

The only ways to be completely safe from sharks are to exterminate them or to stay out of the ocean. Neither option is acceptable to rational people.

As life on land becomes increasingly complex and frustrating, some take pleasure in knowing that the ocean is still an exciting, wild place where they can escape the crowds. It only adds to the sense of adventure knowing that a person can step into the ocean, drop the burden of being the world's most dangerous animal and feel the exquisite alertness that comes from possibly being stalked by a fierce predator with home-field advantage.

I composed and revised many of this book's stories in my mind while surfing alone at dawn in areas patrolled by tiger sharks along O'ahu's North Shore. Because it was the exact worst thing to be thinking about, I used mental gymnastics to rid my mind of troubling thoughts about shark attacks. But the stories were so compelling and the images so vivid, my mind kept returning to the words of the shark-attack victims. So I gave in and worked on the tales, while out of the corner of my eye I thought I spotted shadowy shapes lurking under the water.

Evoking the details of the attacks while alone and far from shore gave me a feeling all too rare to humans, that I was prey. During the lulls between waves, my mind and body were awash in a curious mixture of exhilaration and paralyzing fear.

But the confidence with which the attack victims plunged back into the ocean helped me see the truth in what many experts firmly maintain: the fear of sharks is much greater than the actual danger of being attacked.

I hope that by the time you finish this book you will be inspired by the tales of these brave ocean lovers. And maybe you will come to regard sharks, those beautiful but dangerous and unpredictable creatures, the same way their victims do. With respect instead of fear. ▲

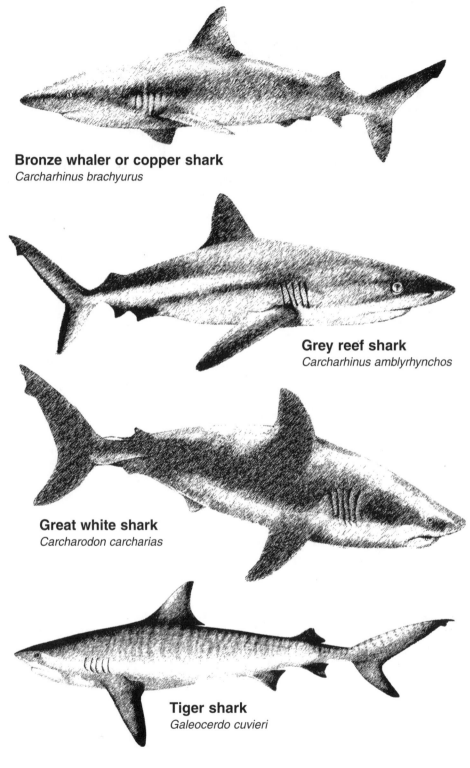

**Bronze whaler or copper shark**
*Carcharhinus brachyurus*

**Grey reef shark**
*Carcharhinus amblyrhynchos*

**Great white shark**
*Carcharodon carcharias*

**Tiger shark**
*Galeocerdo cuvieri*

# Paradise Lost

When Joe Thomson passed the wave-battered cliffs on Kaua'i's north coast and guided his forty-foot yacht into Hanalei Bay, he thought he had sailed into paradise.

It was 1977, and the voyage across the Pacific from central California had been challenging. But Joe's delight in reaching Hanalei was much more than the usual sailor's relief at coming ashore after weeks at sea.

Hanalei Bay is a jewel, a sheltered cove with a white-sand beach that stretches for miles between two points that offer excellent waves for surfers at each end. Coconut palms and ironwood trees line the shore, and wet, green taro fields fill the plain beyond.

The whole area is cut off from the rest of Kaua'i, guarded by towering jagged mountains perpetually capped in clouds and cloaked in verdant foliage. A narrow, rickety metal bridge controls access to Hanalei and the rest of Kaua'i's north shore, and when the Hanalei River floods, the whole area is isolated, to the delight of many who live in the area.

It was the heaven on earth Joe had sought all his life, and he quickly began to explore his new home. He hiked the mountains, discovered hidden waterfall-fed pools, and became well acquainted with the north shore's rugged but exceptionally fine waves.

Slowly, Joe sank roots into the rich, Hawaiian soil and let them spread. He made friends and became a member of the close-knit community. The years passed in sun-drenched splendor, and each day Joe had to pinch himself to confirm that he was really living this dream.

As more people

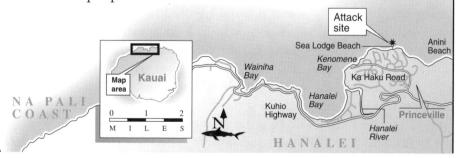

discovered the beauty of the north shore, greater numbers of surfers filled the waves. But Joe didn't mind the crowds. He had discovered his own private playground in his backyard.

The surf spot is called Little Glass Shacks, an ironic reference to the famous Hawaiian song "My Little Grass Shack in Kealakekua, Hawai'i." Only in this case the little grass shack was a rambling mansion filled with windows sitting on the cliff overlooking the surf spot.

Little Glass Shacks is tricky to locate and difficult to reach, at the bottom of a cliff and just offshore of a beach that disappears when large surf surges across the reef and sand to smash against the base of the cliffs.

Joe usually had the place to himself and derived immense satisfaction in being able to catch any wave he wanted without other surfers spoiling his fun. But on October 18, 1985, he encountered "a kind of local that can put a damper on your surf session."

Joe was thirty-three years old and thinking how his life was exceptionally sweet as he looked out the window of his home atop the Princeville cliffs onto a beautiful fall day. The usually wind-chopped ocean was glassy, and four- to six-foot waves were calling to Joe, begging him to come play.

He eagerly walked down the cliff and paddled out on the sleek bodyboard that he had made himself after careful research to create the perfect wave-riding vehicle.

Because he was without his glasses, a trio of green sea turtles got his heart beating quickly when they popped up for air and he couldn't immediately tell if they were friend or foe.

But the waves occupied his full attention, leaving no time to ponder possible predators. Between waves, he bobbed on his board about fifteen feet above the rocky bottom, admiring the beauty of the area and idly wondering what it would look like in twenty years.

Joe turned his thoughts back to the surf and was looking out to sea for another wave with his hands resting over the nose of his board, when suddenly every surfer's worst nightmare engulfed him.

With an explosive whoosh, a large tiger shark erupted from the water and clamped its powerful jaws on the nose of Joe's board. The sharp, serrated teeth easily bit through the nose of the board and sliced through the bone and muscle of Joe's right forearm. Mercifully, the surprise and shock muffled the screaming messages of pain from Joe's nerve endings or he might have fainted from the agony.

It happened so quickly, Joe couldn't believe it really occurred.

One second he was happily anticipating another good ride, and in less than the blink of an eye his hand had disappeared down the tooth-lined maw of Hawai'i's most deadly ocean predator.

Amazingly, as he watched the shark saw through his arm with its jagged teeth, there was still no pain, no sensation of teeth tearing flesh and bone. Joe felt a solid pressure, a crushing sensation, and his hand was gone, vanished into the shark's mouth with a chunk of his body-board.

Joe looked in horror at the safety leash that still attached his arm to his board in the shark's jaws, which dripped with his blood. While Joe floated, stunned and seemingly oblivious to his danger, the creature tore into his board, shaking it ferociously. He still couldn't believe it as he gaped at his right arm: his hand was gone, really gone.

The leash finally slipped off the bloody stump where Joe's hand had been, and that knocked him out of his trance. Finally freed from his death embrace with the shark, Joe kicked furiously with his fins, backing away from the huge predator and those terrible teeth.

Dazed and bleeding but energized by the adrenaline coursing through his veins, Joe couldn't believe his good fortune. It looked as though the shark had forgotten all about him, as it continued to thrash in its battle with the bodyboard. With the shark's full attention focused on the board, Joe kicked his way into the churning white water to try to escape.

But then came the truly terror-filled time for Joe. The attack was so swift and savage that he had reacted instinctively. Now his mind was beginning to betray him as he contemplated swimming the several hundred yards to the safety of shore.

It would have been easiest to swim through the deep water of the channel, but Joe convinced himself the beast was lurking in the deep water, waiting to finish him off.

Fighting to control his fears, Joe swam on his back, propelling himself with his fins and clutching his bleeding stump while calling for help. All the while he frantically scanned the water for the awful sight of the shark. Luckily, a woman on shore heard his cries and rushed to a telephone to summon a rescue team from the police station in nearby Princeville.

Despite losing so much blood, Joe was swimming with strength and confidence thanks to the adrenaline. But his mind was still tormenting him with visions of the shark's bloody jaws ripping into his flesh. Finally, the suspense was unbearable. To make certain the shark wouldn't get another chance to tear him to pieces, Joe climbed on the shallow coral reef to walk to shore, a task made awkward by his swim fins.

It was very slow going, with blood gushing from his wound and his stump throbbing painfully with each faltering step as he tripped over his fins and stepped clumsily into holes in the reef.

He knew he needed help immediately or he would bleed to death, so he reluctantly plunged back into the water, his heart racing with the fear that the shark was following his bloody trail, waiting to pounce. Joe fought the waves of panic that surged within him, using the first-aid training he had recently learned to become a sailboarding instructor.

He realized that the shark wasn't nearly as great a threat as bleeding to death from his severed right hand. Now that he was putting distance between himself and the shark, he looked for other injuries and noticed the creature had slashed his left hand in the attack, and it also was gushing blood.

Joe clamped down on his stump at a pressure point and slowed the bleeding, and continued working his way to shore and help. What seemed like an eternity later, he neared shore and reached Mike Henry, an area resident who was enjoying the solitude of the empty beach. Mike had heard Joe's cries and sprinted to aid the injured surfer.

Highly motivated, Joe outraced Mike across the rocky shore until they reached an area where Mike had left some towels. The two quickly wrapped Joe's wounds and waited for the rescue crew to arrive.

Within minutes, the paramedics stabilized Joe's dreadful wounds and sped off with him in the ambulance for the hourlong ride to Wilcox Memorial Hospital in distant Līhue. The ride passed quickly for Joe, who was pleased to be finally safe from the fearsome tiger shark.

As surgeon Dr. Joseph Conrad Clifford began three hours of surgery to repair Joe's severed right forearm and the torn tendon in his left hand, he put out the word that he could reattach Joe's right hand if it could be found quickly.

An army of volunteers searched the water by boat and shore by foot, but after hours of careful hunting, all they found was Joe's damaged board and the chunk that the shark had ripped from it. Joe's hand had vanished, and he would have to learn how to live without it.

Hours after Dr. Clifford completed his painstaking and delicate surgery, Joe was grateful to be alive, and able to joke about his brush with death. When Dr. Clifford said he would do fine with a double hook prosthesis, Joe quipped that a hook was a wonderful appendage for a sailor.

"I used to play the piano, but I won't be doing that anymore," he added playfully.

When the strong painkillers wore off, the agony that engulfed him was nothing to laugh about. Weeks later, at Halloween, it was all trick and no treat for Joe, who was still in tears from the pain. At times it jolted him hard enough to knock him out of bed. The pain kept him awake until he passed out in exhaustion. Then he slept, until he awakened and the pain quickly overwhelmed him again. His girlfriend, Pam Palmer, was the rock that he clung to for emotional and physical support.

"There were times when I would just break down and cry, and she would hold me and comfort me, and that kept me from wallowing in it longer and longer."

After a few minutes of conversation, it is quickly apparent that Joe is articulate and possesses an inquisitive intellect that is keen to comprehend the workings of everything around him. Yet he is the first to admit that it was lack of awareness that cost him his right hand.

He had been surfing alone, making a much more tempting target for a predator than a group of surfers might have made. A lot of tuna had been swimming along Kaua'i's north shore, which could have attracted sharks into the near-shore waters.

When Joe was attacked, the ocean had been filled with runoff from recent heavy rains, making for poor visibility, which might have led the shark to mistake his bodyboard for a turtle. His yellow-bottomed bodyboard and feet and hands dangling off the ends of his board had completed his unintentional masquerade as a green sea turtle, one of the most common items on a tiger shark's menu.

Hawaiians believe that the area where the tiger shark attacked Joe is the ancestral Kaua'i home of Manō, the shark god. And finally, he had been surfing near the biggest channel in the biggest reef in the Hawaiian Islands. "Was I looking for trouble or what?" he asked.

Months later, by Christmas, Joe was back surfing again, but his life was far from normal. "I was paddling out on a boogie board, no yellow bottom this time. I was just coming around the bowl at Hanalei past the river mouth over the cold water just past the shallow reef.

"A sea turtle popped out of the water right in front of me. He was a little guy, and he never raised his head, so I saw just the back of his shell. It looked just like a shark coming at me. That ruined my day."

Joe paddled another 150 feet toward the surfers in the lineup, then said, "This is no fun anymore," and turned around and paddled back to shore.

"It was a natural thing to want to get back in the water, but there are times and places I didn't want to do it. I didn't want to get struck by lightning twice."

There were victories too. About a year after he lost his hand, Joe was getting ready for a party at Hanalei when he had to decide which hand to wear. He could put on his normal, functional stainless steel grip, or his Gumby hand, a rubber hand painted to look like a real hand, but completely useless. It just has wires inside, and has to be bent to make it move.

"Of course, everyone wants to make the finger out of it. I put on my Gumby hand and said, 'No way, that's not me.' Everyone would say, 'Wow, he grew his hand back.'

"It was a turning point for me, to pick what works over what looks good."

When he's in the ocean, the image of a shark lunging out of the water at him comes forth unbidden from some dark corner of Joe's mind. Some places he gets a vibe and either doesn't go out into the waves or, if he's out surfing when the intuitive warning strikes, heads for shore.

Joe prescribed a dose of world travel to cure himself of his depression and pain, but at times it backfired. Australia was particularly traumatic. He bought a dreamy 2.2-acre parcel of land in a nature preserve in northern New South Wales near a dramatic oceanfront landmark called Broken Head.

"It was a place to die for." But one spooky, stormy day punctuated with lightning bolts and thunderclaps, Joe couldn't keep up with his friends when they paddled around the headland to surf an isolated spot.

He was on a yellow-bottomed bodyboard, and as his friends receded into the gloom, he thought, "I'm not having a good time." Suddenly, a particularly loud thunderclap boomed overhead just as he stroked into a bed of kelp. He nearly died of fright as the touch of the clammy seaweed flooded Joe with images of the shark that attacked him, and every warning alarm began screaming. "I thought,

'I don't want to go through that again.'

"It was like a rite of passage."

Although he loved the unspoiled beauty of the area, Joe never felt comfortable there. During a surf session at Broken Head, a large sea creature sped toward him so rapidly that he couldn't tell it was a dolphin until it was right under him.

But the final straw was talking to area resident and surfing legend George Greenough, who fished the nearby waters regularly. "George said it's so sharky there that it makes him nervous. After losing my hand to a shark, I would sit on the beach and think, 'I'm not going out there.'"

It was time to sell the property and continue his healing journey, to New Zealand, to Asia, to see if he was going to let his fears cripple him.

It helped put things in perspective when he saw Mount Everest on a totally cloudless day. "The mountains were so bloody big, and yet I could see them wrapping around the curve of the Earth and disappearing." Maybe his problems weren't so big after all.

He and Pam got involved with other handicapped people who were worse off than Joe, and he realized that he was inconvenienced rather than handicapped.

They returned to Kaua'i, and Joe confronted his demons. He fished at Little Glass Shacks, but couldn't bring himself to surf there again.

"I've had a number of people tell me that the attack is the gnarliest thing they can think of. But you can't get upset at a wild animal attack."

Joe harbors no grudge against the shark, and he doesn't hate it. "I spent too much time at sea sailing, surfing and fishing to think the shark was doing anything other than what sharks are supposed to do.

"He was looking for dinner, and I was in the wrong place at the wrong time. Why be mad at this big dumb fish, especially when I've eaten so much fish myself?"

He also began speaking in public about the attack. One of his greatest moments was when he spoke to the youngsters at Kīlauea Elementary School on Kaua'i. "For months after that, parents thanked me. They had never had their kids come back from school and talk to their parents about what went on at school that day."

Joe used the story about the shark attack to get their attention, but he had a two-point agenda. One was to teach them how to act around handicapped people. "Kids are fascinated by it. It's right down there at their level. They are so innocent and up-front. I wanted to make them aware of what it means to be handicapped."

The other lesson he wanted to impart was that sooner or later in life, something was going to happen to them, things would go wrong and they would have a real sad time. "And at that point you're going to have a choice. Either be controlled by the event, or take control of the situation and make it better.

"The parents were blown away.

"If someone had told me when I was a young kid, 'It can happen to you, and there are things to watch out for,' I wouldn't have lost my hand. I shouldn't have done what I did that day."

Just when Joe had taken charge of his life, another act of nature knocked things beyond his control.

On September 11, 1992, Hurricane 'Iniki slammed into Kaua'i and scattered people's lives and dreams. Joe looked at the devastated island and decided it was time to make another change.

He returned to California to go to school and sharpen his talents as a graphic artist. He was a fair hand with an airbrush long before he ever moved to Hawai'i, and he has become a great hand with a computer.

He still surfs, haunting the California coast between the Hollister Ranch and Ventura, and he still makes bodyboards, but with black bottoms that might not look so tempting to sharks.

And he suggests that surfers might be wise to break up the color of their surfboard bottom with stickers so they look less like prey, and maybe even paint a large mouth to make it look like another shark.

Joe also has kept busy building the perfect mechanical hand. It's only a prototype, but it does everything he wants it to. It's considered too unorthodox for anyone to invest in, but that's okay. Joe is content to use a hand built by Bob Radocy, a one-handed friend who lives in Boulder, Colorado. It's a perfectly pragmatic hand, built by an amputee for amputees.

Bob's hand is wonderfully simple, a series of crescent shapes in a prehensile grip that twists and opens and closes to hold objects of different sizes. Joe is unimpressed with the latest technological prosthetic wonders, complicated devices that work marvelously but are impossible to repair when they inevitably break down at an inconvenient time and place.

Joe doesn't feel that he's working at a disadvantage in his new profession as a graphic artist because a shark took his right hand. "Computers for the most part already have a Napoleon complex, especially for graphics, when you use a mouse with only one hand a lot."

Joe's life is richer and more satisfying than ever, and except for the occasional speaking engagement to the Santa Barbara Surf Club or other similar groups, he hardly ever talks about the shark that took his right hand and part of his forearm.

Sometimes, though, he can't resist. "I've had a number of amputees ask me what happened, and when I tell them, they say, 'Gosh, I wish I could tell that story.' Many of them got drunk and crashed their car into something and were responsible for their own problem."

Despite the passage of time, people are still fascinated by the story of Joe's attack. "After this long, it has been interesting to see how people react to what to them is very heavy news." Joe can even create a sensation without mentioning the attack.

"I went to see *Robocop* when it first came out, and I thought it was pretty cool. When the movie was over, we went out the side door. Pam was in front, and because the person in front let the door go, as it started to close I thrust my hand out to stop it. It was a metal door, and I had on my metal hand, so it made a huge metallic noise. This little old lady behind me freaked. Right after *Robocop*, here's this guy whacking doors open."

The attack still lingers in Joe's mind, but he has long since made his peace with it. Kaua'i sits as his ace in the hole, and the surf will always be there in front of his jungle-covered piece of property near where his life was changed forever.

"Certainly one of the apex experiences of my life will always be the shark attack, and especially the aftereffects. It changed my living patterns and exposed me to other things.

"It's like Hurricane 'Iniki was. The storm itself was pretty bad, but the hard part was living with the aftereffects. In some ways it added to my life, in that instead of being so thoroughly involved in the ocean, now I've done other things.

"The ocean is a highlight of my life rather than a focal point. There is always going to be another day of surf."

With a mischievous grin, he adds, "It would be a really neat experience to have had if I didn't get hurt." ▲

# Just Another Nightmare

As with all things too terrible to endure, the nightmares finally stopped months after sixteen-year-old Greg Filtzer watched a shark slash a fellow surfer's arm to pieces in Mexico.

Over the years, Greg pushed that grim memory into the far recesses of his mind. During fifteen years spent fishing for a living, Greg stopped thinking of sharks as bloodthirsty demons, and they became just another fish in his watery world. Because there was no profit in catching them, they weren't even very interesting fish to him.

By the time he was forty-three, Greg thought of sharks only when the occasional newspaper headline briefly caught his attention after some poor surfer or swimmer suffered a painful encounter with a shark.

But on October 15, 1990, Greg suddenly became extremely interested in sharks again.

The day was custom designed for surfing. The sun was shining in a brilliant blue sky, the waves were good, and the water was warm. Predictably, the main break at Hanalei Point on Kaua'i's north shore was crowded with surfers, so Greg took his brother-in-law, Robert Duhe, to a less-crowded area around the point.

Greg called the spot Summerland, and it was his haven from the frustrations created by too many surfers competing for too few waves at Hanalei Point. Although the waves at Summerland weren't nearly as good as the perfect long, peeling walls that made Hanalei Point internationally famous, the lack of aggressive surfers made it a guaranteed pleasure zone.

It was about three in the afternoon, and the surf session was a highlight

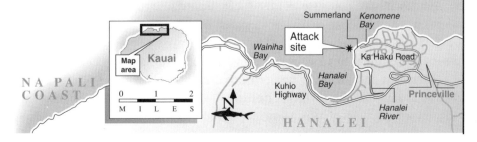

of Robert's visit from California. Robert enjoyed the freedom of surfing without a wet suit, a necessity in California, and savored the sensation of the sun warming his skin while the cool ocean caressed his bare legs.

The two laughed as they shared the waves, hooting at each other's rides and chuckling over the wipeouts. Between waves, Greg enjoyed pointing out interesting landmarks of this lovely stretch of coast that had captured his heart, from the cliffs beneath Princeville to the long, sandy beach that ended where the waves peeled at Waikoko's on the far west end of Hanalei Bay.

Life couldn't be any better, and Robert and Greg hoped that the rest of their lives would be filled with such splendid moments. They spotted an approaching set of waves, and as they positioned themselves to intercept them, something slammed into Greg so violently that he felt as though he was sitting in his car at a stoplight and another car plowed into him.

The impact stunned Greg, but his mind quickly cleared and he realized with horror that a powerful creature had rammed him. He never saw the creature coming, but the attack was strong and deliberate, as though a predator was checking to see what kind of meal Greg would make.

Before he could react to that knowledge and try to escape, the beast bit into the tail of Greg's nine-foot surfboard and began pulling the board and rider underwater. Greg was facing away from his attacker, lying prone on his board, and his already considerable fear was heightened by the fact that he couldn't see his tormentor. His imagination ran wild, filling his mind with visions of the ocean's most horrible monsters.

He could hear the terrible sound of teeth gnawing on his surfboard, and his terror at ending up in the water with his attacker boosted Greg's strength. He clung ferociously to his surfboard and began climbing to the nose of the board to get as far from the gnashing teeth as possible.

He soon was at the end of his board, and the mystery beast seemed determined to make a meal of him. The powerful animal pulled Greg backward in a circle and began shaking the board violently, causing him to increase his already intense grip.

Terrified by the huge unseen creature that was trying to pull him down into the cold, dark depths, Greg's mind was flooded by unwanted images of the nightmarish shark attack he had witnessed

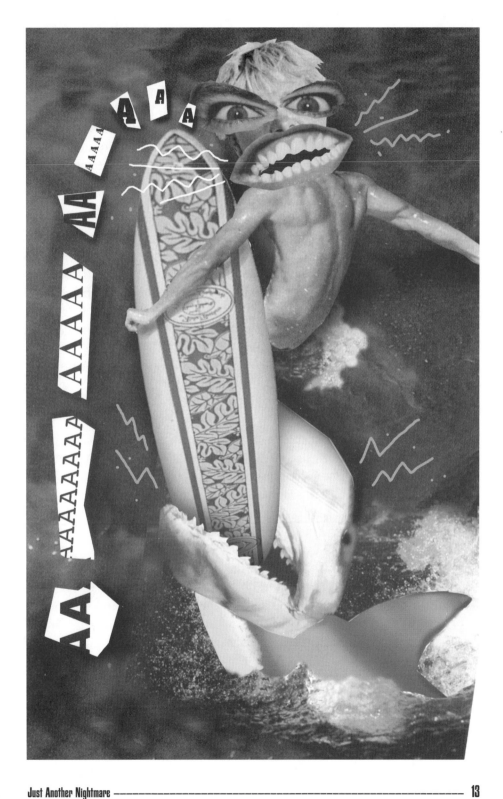

as a youth, images that had been buried for decades. He was convinced he was about to be eaten alive.

His brother-in-law watched in horror and resisted the tremendous urge to rapidly paddle his surfboard to the safety of the beach 250 yards away. Many people would have tried to save their own skins, but Robert stayed to help out if he could, even though he was beginning to think the creature might turn on him at any moment.

Greg was too busy fighting for his life to appreciate Robert's loyalty. He was taking a deep breath, getting ready to be pulled under with his unseen attacker and battle with it under the waves. And then the creature's powerful jaws snapped the tail off Greg's surfboard, the violent movement of his surfboard ceased, and Greg was bobbing on his board wondering what was going to happen next.

He couldn't stand the suspense, so he twisted his head to peer over his shoulder and get a good look at the brute that had been savaging his board. Greg was amazed to see the thick, wide body of a tiger shark of incredible girth. It looked about twelve feet long, and massive enough to swallow Greg whole.

The tiger shark rolled its huge gray body in an easy motion and swam off with the piece of surfboard in its mouth, and Greg's awe of the creature was replaced by a sickening awareness of just how far he was from shore.

Greg had a steel-crushing grip on his mutilated surfboard, convinced that the shark was preparing to return and continue its assault and that he would need to wield his board as a shield from the shark's flashing teeth. Curiously, Greg was as calm as the eye of a storm. He was coming off an adrenaline rush, his body was in shock, and he was completely limp. Nothing could have bothered him; Greg had looked death in the eye, and survived.

But the shark was still out there, and once it tired of chewing on the surfboard chunk it might come back for something more tasty, so Greg and Robert beat a hasty retreat for the beach.

As the shock wore off during the long paddle to shore, Greg's mind cleared and he appreciated how close he had come to death, and he was grateful to be alive. "There is nothing more violent than being eaten alive by a wild animal. When they eat you, they screw around with you for a while. They chew on you, spit you out, and mess around with you."

By the time Greg finally reached the beach and felt truly safe from the shark, he realized that this was a crucial moment in his life. He went to his nearby home, grabbed his wife's surfboard and paddled the two-mile length of Hanalei Bay to work the experience out of his system. "I knew that if I didn't do that, it would be hard to get back into it. The long, hard paddle had a calming effect on my psyche.

"I feel bad for anybody that this happens to. The worst thing that could happen is for it to turn you away from the ocean."

Once he worked through his fears, Greg began to worry about how his four children would react. His biggest enjoyment in life was to surf with his wife and kids, and he didn't want the attack to make them afraid of the ocean.

With his shark-scarred surfboard visible in the yard, Greg gathered his children and tried to put the incident into perspective. He explained to them that the ocean is the shark's environment, and at certain times they shouldn't be in the ocean.

It worked. His kids are avid surfers, and they all trust their intuition when they get a feeling that sharks are on the prowl. Their reaction has been a dream come true for Greg. But there were unexpected aftershocks that Greg couldn't exorcise with physical exertion or calm logic.

While on a surfari to Mexico in the sixties, Greg had just paddled in from a good surf session when he paused to watch a surfer stroking for a set wave. He was astounded to see a shark streak up, grab the surfer's arm and rip it to shreds. It terrified him, and he never surfed that spot again. "It was really a horrible thing; the shark turned that guy's arm to hamburger."

After his own attack on Kaua'i, the long-forgotten images tormented him. "For me to see that, and then years later be attacked, I flashed heavy on it that night after I was home. I relived that whole experience too, so vividly, like I was just there."

Nights became a terrible time for Greg, not always, but often enough to make his life miserable. He had nightmares for months, intense images that haunted his sleep, sometimes fantastic, sometimes realistic, always violent scenes where he was attacked by the shark again.

Finally, he looked up fellow Kaua'i resident Joe Thomson, who in 1985 was attacked by a tiger shark a few miles from where Greg was hit. The big tiger shark ripped off Joe's right hand and forearm and mauled his left hand.

"I introduced myself and we had a long chat. He was way worse off than me, in serious mental and physical pain. He really helped me put things into perspective."

Slowly, the nightmares faded, and now they trouble Greg's sleep only occasionally. The incident doesn't intrude on his daydreams either. "I haven't thought about it in a long time."

In fact, there has been no long-term trauma from the attack. Greg has been firmly addicted to the pleasures of surfing for forty years, and no shark attack was going to keep him from the waves.

He surfs as much as he ever did, and although he isn't afraid of sharks, he's more aware that they are out there. But the fear of sharks doesn't keep him from his favorite surf spot. It's the humans that have chased him away.

"The only reason I don't surf the backside of Hanalei Point, where I was attacked, is the crowds of surfers. When I grew up surfing, there was protocol. That protocol is long gone. These days it's 'I, me, mine.'"

Some Hawai'i residents have taken it personally when sharks attacked them and have sought vengeance against the creatures by calling for state or private shark hunts. But Greg had no such thoughts. "I was in his environment. He was doing what comes natural. I was in the wrong place at the wrong time. He got a fiberglass sandwich instead of a taste of me, and I never saw him again. He didn't want me."

Greg feels that the only reason the sharks are a problem where he lives is because of the commercial fishing boats, which lure the predators into Hanalei Bay late in the summer and early fall when they fish for *akule* in the bay. They load their nets until they are filled, and when they dump their nets the unwanted fish end up floating in the bay.

"Invariably, we end up with a lot of shark activity in the bay. My wife and I witnessed a shark feeding frenzy, with three or four areas of sharks going nuts on the dead *akule*, rolling over in it and jumping in it."

Such a feeding frenzy almost tragically ended a honeymooning couple's brief marriage. It was their first day in Hawai'i, and Hanalei Bay provided the perfect romantic backdrop for their dream trip. The newlyweds were enchanted by the warm tropical ocean and the quaint little town of Hanalei, with the mysterious, jagged green mountains looming over this slice of paradise. They were equally tempted to walk the long beach that stretched invitingly the length of Hanalei Bay, or swim in the calm ocean that was clad in the most delightful shades of turquoise. The ocean was irresistible, so they went for a swim, stroking playfully side by side across the bay.

They had no way of knowing that the *akule* boats had recently dumped their nets, leaving dead *akule* floating in the water and lining the shore. And the sharks were busy gorging themselves on the free banquet.

"They were just doing what they thought was a fun thing to do, but they were swimming directly toward these sharks," says Greg, shuddering at the memory. "My friend and I paddled out on longboards, put them on our boards and paddled them back in. We showed them the sharks, and they were in shock. They had been thirty yards away from six sharks eating in one area. I have no doubts that it could have been an ugly situation.

"I felt bad for them. It was their first introduction to Hawai'i." ▲

# Never Surf Alone Again

Like most Kaua'i surfers, Jude Chamberlin is rugged. You have to be to surf Kaua'i's waves. The reefs are shallow and sharp, the waves powerful, the surf spots isolated. It's no place for the weak of mind or body, and Jude is neither.

Her favorite spot is Cannon's, near the end of the road at Hā'ena on Kaua'i's north shore. It's a nasty spot with a punishing, hollow wave. Surfers who hesitate or make the slightest mistake are slammed onto the reef, and many bear interesting scars as mute testimony to the surf spot's ferocity.

Jude loves the place. Her preferred tactic is to paddle out in the dark at the first hint of dawn, to surf in delicious solitude.

Jude and her friend Mike Cox were excited at the prospect of good waves as they walked up the beach to check the surf at Cannon's on March 28, 1992. The sun was sending a first few tentative rays over the mountains, and it was already obvious that this was the kind of Hawaiian winter day that people on the mainland dream about before waking up to another blizzard.

The ocean was seventy-two degrees, the air was seventy-two degrees, and there wasn't a cloud to be seen. The water was clear and there were no green sea turtles bobbing offshore for algae, none of the usual indicators that sharks might be prowling the ocean.

Jude was ready to hit the waves immediately, but at 6:45 a light breeze began to ruf-
fle the ocean's surface,
and Mike decid-

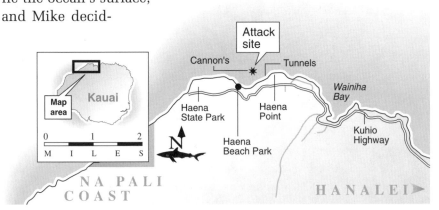

ed that the wind was going to strengthen and ruin the waves. "More waves for me," Jude thought as Mike headed home.

Another friend arrived and paddled out to Tunnels a few hundred yards away while Jude stroked out to surf Cannon's alone.

The anticipated wind never arrived to chop out the waves, and Jude was pleased to see Mike return to join her in the lineup. After catching a particularly satisfying wave, Jude eagerly stroked back out, anticipating a good morning of surf.

She had skirted the shallow coral and headed through the keyhole-shaped channel of deeper water when she felt her board starting to lift. Annoyed at the interruption, she thought to herself, "Stupid turtle." But when she looked over her shoulder for the culprit that had thrown her off course, she saw something gray hovering over her legs.

She still didn't realize her danger, thinking a big fish was swimming over her. As she looked more intently at the intruder, Jude was horrified to see that it was a large tiger shark, Hawai'i's most dangerous predator. The shark's mouth was gaping wide, exposing rows of nasty, serrated teeth poised to clamp down on Jude's legs.

Sick with fear, Jude watched in a trance as the terrible jaws bit down on her legs. Although her mind was buzzing with terror, one small corner of her brain wondered in fascination why she couldn't feel the hooked teeth tearing into her flesh. The answer came in a lightning bolt: one of her surfboard's three fins must have stuck in the tiger's bottom jaw, preventing the shark from biting through her board and chewing off her leg.

Her brief elation was vaporized by the certainty that the shark's deadly intentions were merely momentarily thwarted, and it would still find a way to get her. Jude clung to her surfboard, her only refuge from the terrifying creature as the great gray shark struggled mightily to close its jaws completely. As it twisted and thrashed, the shark tilted the surfboard, breaking Jude's grip and tossing her from the safe platform. The situation could scarcely be worse. She was in the water with the carnivore as it swung her surfboard like a cat shaking a mouse.

Jude watched the shark thrash her surfboard until the creature did a belly roll and swam away, still chomping on the board. Just as she dared to think that the attack might be over, Jude was yanked after the shark by her leash, which was still attached to her surfboard and her ankle. Jude stroked and kicked furiously to hold her position,

but her efforts were futile as the powerful shark dragged her sixty feet through the water.

Jude was desperate to untie the leash to escape the shark, but she dreaded making any move that might divert its attention from the surfboard to her. She was in a terrible situation, still being dragged by the shark and unable to free herself. She couldn't force herself to put her head under the water to watch the shark; the sight of the tiger turning to attack her would have been unbearable. Luckily, the shark had dragged her into water shallow enough that it couldn't pull her under.

Finally, frantic and endless minutes later, her leash went slack, but it brought no comfort to Jude. She was convinced the shark had tired of battling the surfboard and was circling back to get her, and she was helpless in the water with nothing to shield her from the shark's hideous teeth. Jude felt like a little girl again, and the ultimate bogeyman was about to leap out from under the bed and pounce on her.

And then, to her immense relief, her surfboard popped up from the ocean's depths. Even though it meant possibly swimming straight into the shark's waiting jaws, Jude churned the water in her haste to retrieve the board. Safely aboard her battered board, Jude yelled to Mike that she was heading over the reef.

The deep channel is the usual safe route around the jagged coral, but she already had spent far too much time in the channel with the tiger shark. Jude didn't fully realize what had just happened until she was standing on the shallow reef, finally free from her tormentor. As the sharp coral sliced her feet, Jude began counting to make sure both were still attached to her legs. Then she saw the blood dripping off her surfboard. Minutes earlier she had been too busy fighting for her life for the full impact to register, but now her mind swirled with images of the shark.

Her body shook as the adrenaline worked its way through her system. Jude savored the sweet feeling of being alive, and took a moment to appreciate the terrible fate she had just escaped. "You think that when you're in the water is when you would really freak out," she says. Standing on the reef, Jude watched numbly as blood from her bitten foot dripped into the water and mingled with blood dripping off the surfboard, her blood that had been in the shark's jaws.

Aware that the shark easily could have mangled her, Jude was dumbstruck, unable to speak to another surfer paddling out and warn him of the shark that might still be lurking in the channel.

Jude had no way of knowing yet that the shark had taken something very special from her.

Limp from emotional exhaustion, Jude made her way to shore, where Mike joined her on the beach, proud that he hadn't abandoned her to bolt for safety. "I stayed out with you. I was going to pull the torso in," Mike told her.

When she got her wits about her, Jude knew that she had to get in the water right away or she might develop an aversion to the ocean, and at thirty-six, she had far too many good days of surf ahead of her to be afraid of the water. So she insisted that they drive to Hanalei to surf the lefts at Waikoko's.

The next morning she went back to Cannon's, but something was different. "I wanted it to feel like it always was, but it was really eerie, and always is now." She paddled rapidly past the place where she had been attacked and joined her friends in the lineup. When a Hawaiian monk seal popped up nearby, Jude came totally unglued, and started frantically stroking for shore until her friends grabbed her and calmed her down, saying, "See, it's only a seal."

She tried to surf Cannon's the next few days alone, but she couldn't enjoy herself. It just wasn't fun. Years after the attack, Jude still paddles out at dawn to surf alone. But not at Cannon's. Never at Cannon's.

"I'm not a fearful kind of person," says Jude. "I went out there about ten times to surf it alone, but I couldn't get past myself. I would start looking around, thinking of teeth and jaws, and go in.

"When I'm surfing now, if my hand hits a stick in the water or a turtle pops up, I jump out of my skin. Before, it was never a problem. If I saw something in the water, I never thought it was a shark.

"I wish it wasn't like that. I surf every day, but there is no making it go away.

"When I go out with a friend at Cannon's, I try to paddle past that spot."

She also occasionally dreams about the shark, but in her dreams it's not an attack, it's a battle. "It's always a bigger shark, it's biting me and I'm punching it and we're having a big match in the water."

People asked her if she didn't want to round up volunteers and hunt down the shark, but that was never an option. "There are so many things people have tried to get rid of because they don't like them, and screwed things up even worse," Jude says.

"I guess I needed the drama. I got a free surfboard, some free meals, a TV spot," she says, laughing.

"I do more thinking on it now than at the time. I reminisce, and I think, 'What if I lost my leg? My whole life would be different.' It would have taken away the best thing in my life, surfing."

Mike wasn't so fortunate. Although he wasn't attacked, watching Jude fight for her life was a nightmare come true for him. "He used to be terrified of sharks as a kid in Florida," says Jude. "He used to surf every day, but he hardly surfs anymore.

"Once it gets you, you can't stop thinking about it in the lineup. Things can be going great, and once my mind gets ahold of that thought, I'm shot. I can't get it out of my mind." ▲

# Mother Knows Best

As she stood on the beach at Hanalei on Kauaʻi's north shore, Kathleen Lunn was convinced that November 13, 1994, was destined to be a very special day. Her family and friends were going for a fun surf session at Hanalei Point, and later in the day the surf club to which her children belonged was going to meet and surf with three-time world champion surfer Tom Curren. The reward for the best surfers in the group might be a sponsorship from Australian wet suit company Rip Curl.

If Kathleen was excited about the meeting, her three children, Stephen, twelve, Koral, fourteen, and Melanie, sixteen, were delirious with anticipation. Tom Curren was handsome, soft-spoken yet articulate, confident yet humble, a good musician and a surfer who could carve a flourish on the waves with a subtle grace and flamboyant style imitated worldwide by surfers young and old. And he was the only surfer in history to have recaptured the world title while surfing the world tour as a wild card competitor.

Her children's enthusiasm was contagious, and just before ten A.M., as they all began the long paddle out to the waves at Hanalei Point, Kathleen was convinced she was going to have a great surf session.

But along the way, her intuition began to erode her confidence. Nothing ever surfaced as a conscious thought, but deep in the back of her mind something was whispering a warning. As she approached the area where the Hanalei River empties into the bay, the feeling had deepened into a sense of dread.

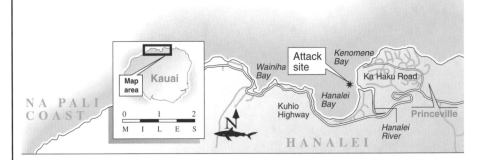

She had the jitters, which was odd, because Kathleen was always completely at ease in the ocean and rode the waves with confidence born of the tremendous pleasure surfing gave her. She stopped paddling and looked around to find the source of her psychic discomfort, but nothing was amiss around her.

The Hanalei River drains one of the most fertile basins in Hawai'i, an area of lush taro fields, vast wetlands that shelter endangered water birds, and mountains that wring an impressive amount of moisture out of the tropical clouds.

The river flushes an amazing variety of flora and fauna into the ocean at the east end of Hanalei Bay. Surfers heading for Hanalei Point must paddle through the murky water of the river mouth to reach the long, fast waves out at the point.

Sometimes the river delivers the surfers a surprise, usually nothing more than a dead critter that has floated downstream, or fish splashing unexpectedly in the silt-laden water.

With a mother's pride, Kathleen looked at her children several dozen yards closer to the action, duck diving their surfboards under breaking waves on the inside section. Kathleen had stroked past the river mouth and was in thirty feet of water on the edge of the channel paddling over the shoulder of a wave, when she felt something lift her surfboard. Although she was still in the silted plume of the river flow and couldn't see her own hands in the water, a sixth sense told her immediately that she hadn't hit a submerged tree or branch in the water. Whatever she had hit was large, and alive.

Before she could take another stroke, a large shape emerged from the murk and bit into the right side of her board and her thigh. Kathleen was facing forward while paddling and couldn't get a good look at the creature, which only heightened her fears as she wondered what in the world had a hold of her. She was only thirty-four years old, and she wasn't about to let some predator take her.

Her immediate reaction was to wrench her thigh from the creature's mouth, and then another, stronger instinct kicked in and overcame the fear that was welling up inside of her.

She looked over at her children and other youngsters from the surf club paddling nearby, their attention focused on the waves and oblivious to the attack. A fierce mother's instinct to protect her children made her forget about her own safety, and kindled a fury within her. Kathleen sat up on the tail of her nine-foot surfboard and lashed out with her board at the mysterious creature.

"You're not going to get my family," she thought as she felt her board deliver a satisfyingly solid blow to her attacker in the murky water. It worked. The swift counterattack sent the creature fleeing, providing Kathleen only a glimpse as it dove into the cloudy depths. Whatever it was, the beast was as long as her surfboard.

The others had been busy ducking their surfboards under approaching waves and missed the attack, except for one youngster on a bodyboard who saw Kathleen whacking at some large animal in the water. He swiftly turned around and paddled urgently for the beach.

She paddled over to her kids and told them she thought she might have been bitten by a shark, and they quickly started following her to shore. She also told some of the nearly forty surfers in the lineup of the attack, but they all decided the waves were worth the risk and stayed out surfing.

Still in a protective mode, Kathleen was eager to herd her group to the safety of shore and didn't waste time examining her aching thigh or her surfboard. She wasn't willing to accept the fact that she had been attacked by a shark, and especially didn't want to panic the kids. As she paddled, Kathleen began to quietly question herself about what had just happened.

Maybe it was just a crazy dolphin or a barracuda, she thought. But she abandoned that wishful thinking as soon as she reached knee-deep water and began walking toward shore. She saw the perfect crescent shape of bite gouges on the top and bottom of her board, and she at last admitted to herself that a large tiger shark had targeted her for a meal.

She briefly considered the tiger shark's fearsome reputation and was immediately relieved to have escaped so easily. "Wow, I'm so glad I've still got my leg," she said to herself.

People in the parking lot made a big commotion as soon as they spotted her bleeding thigh and tooth-tattered board. To her utter amazement, in an effort to make Kathleen feel better some men pulled up their shirts to show off scars from their shark encounters. A great white shark savagely assaulted Kenny Doudt in 1979 while he was surfing in Oregon's frigid waters. He moved to Hawai'i to enjoy the islands' warmer waves and splendid shortage of great white sharks. "I know you're in shock," Kenny told Kathleen as he lifted his shirt to reveal his hideous souvenir from the great white.

His gesture of empathy worked. Kathleen immediately forgot her

own harrowing attack and felt sorry for Kenny. Then another surfer who had been bitten in the side by a shark raised his shirt and showed off his gigantic scar, and Kathleen immediately felt sorry for him, too.

In fact, she was becoming embarrassed that she hadn't been horribly mutilated, but she got over that as soon as she realized the ridiculousness of such a thought.

Drained by the emotional encounter, Kathleen just wanted to go home and take care of the wound herself, but her husband insisted that they had to report it to the police at the Hanalei fire station. The firemen treated the two-inch-wide wound and suggested that the couple drive to distant Wilcox Hospital near Līhuʻe so doctors could stitch it up.

When police officers went down to the beach at Hanalei to try to clear the surfers out of the water for their own safety, they were amazed that half of them refused to leave the surf, and those that came to shore paddled back out immediately when they saw the others catching the suddenly uncrowded waves.

It took a lot of persuading to get Kathleen to agree to go to the hospital. It was at least an hour's drive from Hanalei, and she didn't want to risk missing the meeting with Tom Curren at Hanalei Surf Company.

She need not have worried. The doctor quickly stitched the wound closed and made her feel luckier than she already felt by remarking that the last person he had patched after a shark attack needed 240 stitches.

When she walked into the surf shop for the meeting, there were one hundred people waiting for her. She was the talk of the gathering and stole the show from Tom Curren.

Because Kathleen had reacted to the attack with such nonchalance, her kids reacted really well, too. She had spent years calming their fears, bandaging their injuries, and instilling in them a love of the ocean. She wasn't going to let some shark undo all her hard work.

The whole group of youngsters went off to surf a known sharky area with Tom Curren, and Kathleen's son Stephen so impressed Tom with his surfing ability that he signed the lad to surf for the Rip Curl team.

But although she was at ease with the attack during daylight hours, something deeper within wasn't settled. Kathleen was so intent on protecting her kids from being emotionally scarred by the attack that she hadn't allowed herself to come to terms with the dreadful encounter. And so the shark visited Kathleen in her dreams.

In one, the shark was coming at her, and she shouted "No!" and woke up. "It's just like a vicious dog is coming at you. You don't just stand there and let it bite you, you push it away. You're supposed to show them who's boss."

By the time her stitches were removed two weeks later, she was back surfing again. It was just the physically and emotionally cleansing tonic she needed, and the shark dreams vanished, never to return.

Kathleen came to regard the attack as a blessing, because her kids figured that their mom had used up all the bad luck with sharks so they would never be harmed. They weren't bothered by the attack, but other people were, including one woman friend who didn't go in the water for a long time after the incident.

"I have more respect for sharks now," Kathleen says. "I love animals, dolphins, whales, birds. I never really liked sharks because they have such a bad reputation. I feel for them; they get killed way more than us.

"I always used to say that if you see a shark, you're lucky. My kids remind me of that. I have the prettiest little scar, like the Hawaiians used to have tattooed on their ankles to keep them from being bitten by sharks. Hawaiians say the shark is my *'aumakua* (guardian) now."

Kathleen is constantly putting her *'aumakua* to the test. Because of the kids, she and her husband surf the dawn patrol, supposedly a time when sharks are very active. "They are always in the water swimming around under you. It's their home. We surf a lot of sharky spots with no problem."

The kids have excelled in the years since the attack. Stephen won the boys and junior state amateur titles, Melanie is the number one female amateur surfer, and all three get straight A's in school.

And mom is enjoying the ocean more than ever after the attack. "When it hasn't happened, you worry about it happening. But once it happens, you don't worry about it anymore.

"I knew there was something wrong. I had just told somebody I have stage fright today, and I never have stage fright in the ocean. It happened right after that. You get a little premonition because your body is going into that fight or flight mode, but people don't pay attention to that instinct anymore.

"If you feel there is something wrong, there probably is, so you better react to it." ▲

# More Than a Prayer of a Chance

Roddy Lewis has always felt at home in the ocean. It was a dividend of growing up on the windward side of O'ahu, fishing, diving and surfing in two of Hawai'i's finest ocean playgrounds.

Kāne'ohe, the largest bay in the state, is filled with fish and exquisite coral formations that grow to incredible shapes in the bay's calm waters. And nearby Kailua offers fun waves and a long beach coated with sand soft enough that someone clever could have made a fortune using it to cushion the soles of jogging shoes.

Roddy was content with all the ways he found to extract fun from the ocean. But when he discovered sailboarding, it changed his life forever. It was a miracle to be able to fill his rig's sail with wind and fly across the water, to feel his arms flex as he manipulated the boom and mast to make the board go ever faster.

Sure, it was fun to hit the little waves at Jump City in Kailua Bay at full steam and get launched into the air, creating ever so briefly the illusion of flight. But Roddy was a speed junkie. No matter how hard he tried, he couldn't outrun his need to go faster and faster, until he was just a blur across the water.

Kailua offers fine flat water and stiff trade winds, but anyone who is serious about setting his sailboard in motion knows that Maui is magic.

Roddy moved to Maui and found the perfect place for a sailboarding fiend: Kū'au, on Maui's north shore. The tiny little town is a speck on the Hāna Highway, and tourists leaving colorful Pā'ia to zoom off toward heavenly Hāna can easily blink and miss the country store that marks Kū'au.

But Kū'au is the epicenter of world-class

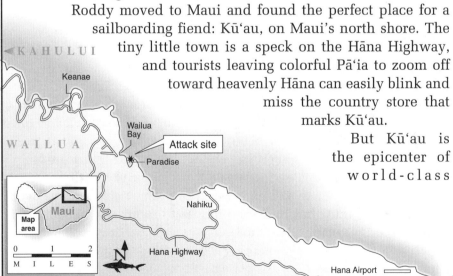

sailboarding, a magnet that attracts fanatical boardsailors from across the globe.

With exceptional waves in his own backyard, Roddy could carry his rig across a small beach and set sail. A few hundred yards east is Hoʻokipa Beach Park, where the consistent trade winds blow in fun summer surf perfect for practicing wave-jumping. In winter, fierce storms create fearsome waves that tower over the sailboard masts and threaten to pummel the riders, who laugh and perform daring aerials and other acrobatics as they defy the menacing waves.

But Roddy's main pleasure zone lay a few miles west of Kūʻau, at Spreckelsville, named after a powerful sugarcane baron. Northeast trade winds blast across thousands of miles of open ocean to hit Spreckelsville at just the right angle to let sailboarders blaze across the shallow water.

At Spreckelsville Roddy could fill his sails with the howling trade winds and head for the horizon like a bat out of hell, then jibe and double his speed on the way back. With the perfect training ground, Roddy's already impressive skills quickly became daunting. He speared fish to supplement his income as a carpenter, a job that left him plenty of time to sail when the winds were shrieking. Before long, he was winning speed-sailing contests and setting his sights on competition abroad.

His carpentry work and constant sailing shaped Roddy into a six-foot four-inch pillar of steel, and he felt invincible as he sped across the water. But there were times when encounters in the ocean touched him with a feeling of mortal dread.

Late one afternoon off Kanahā bird sanctuary, the wind was so perfect that Roddy couldn't resist making one more run, even though the sun had long since ducked behind majestic Haleakalā and darkness threatened to descend quickly.

He was blazing along when he caught the top of a swell and soared into the air. Suspended in midair, he spotted a big, bulky shadow directly below him. To his horror, Roddy realized it was a huge tiger shark, with a head wider than his sailboard. He was on a collision course with a beast that was at least twenty feet long.

Roddy used some inspired gymnastics to narrowly miss the shark, and as darkness snatched the light from the sky he sped back to the beach, his mind filled with images of the enormous shark racing after him.

Over the next few days Roddy almost convinced himself the incident was a trick his mind had played on him with help from the twilight. How could there be a monster tiger shark haunting waters that he sailed so frequently?

While talking story with a fisherman, he cautiously mentioned the giant shark, certain the man would scoff at the tale. Instead, the fisherman casually said it sounded like the gigantic shark that often shadowed his crew's twenty-four-foot outrigger canoe when they paddled outside Kahului Harbor.

Slowly, great days of sailing and surfing replaced the memory of the giant tiger shark. Not content to burn grooves in the ocean sailing back and forth at Spreckelsville, Roddy continually sought greater challenges. He and a friend stared across an intimidating expanse of water to barely visible Maui as they rigged up their boards and set sail from the Big Island's Kohala Coast, taking aim at Mākena on Maui's southwest shore.

Their course took them straight across the melodically named 'Alenuihāhā Channel, a rough stretch of ocean buffeted by fierce winds and tossed by chaotic seas. After hours of strenuous sailing, they were about six miles off Maui and startled a bottomfisherman when they sailed up out of nowhere and swooped past his boat.

After that bit of amusement, the duo tried to do some serious sailing to reach Maui's southwest shore. The crossing was more difficult than they had anticipated, and the sun was hovering just above the horizon. They were two miles off La Perouse Bay, a sparsely populated area with a coastline guarded by jagged lava. It was no place to attempt a blind landing in the dark.

Just as his sails picked up a solid breeze to let Roddy beat the darkness to shore, he was slammed by a tornado of swirling winds that churned the ocean into a maelstrom and ripped the boom right out of his hands.

Roddy went down hard, and every time he tried to set sail the howling wind knocked him flat again. He shouted to warn his friend, but the wind carried his warning away and the hellish storm crumpled his partner.

As the dark curtain of night dropped over the ocean, they decided to roll up their rigging and paddle for La Perouse Bay. Despite his best efforts to entertain more-cheerful thoughts, images of the shadowy tiger came flooding back, and Roddy wondered how many other giant tiger sharks prowled these waters.

An eternity later they reached shore in pitch black and painfully walked barefoot across the jagged lava. The pack of ten flares in their survival kit was soggy, and the flares sputtered and died until the very last one caught fire and blazed a rescue beacon.

The same bottomfisherman they had surprised earlier was heading home when he spotted the flare, and as he took the sailboarders to Mākena they entertained him with their tale of woe. They were already cold from exposure, but the fisherman chilled their hearts when he told them of the six-hundred-pound tiger shark he had caught right where they had floundered in the storm.

Whether atop the waves or beneath the surface, the ocean was Roddy's playground and his pantry. Surfing and sailboarding nourished his soul, while fishing nurtured his body. In the dark, wave-tossed waters off Maui's isolated north shore, Roddy was spearfishing for his dinner when a Galapagos shark swam out of the deep and gave Roddy the black-death stare with its merciless eye.

Roddy surprised himself by staring the shark down, though he had his spear tip ready to poke the predator if his glowering expression hadn't sent the shark on its way.

The threat of lurking sharks wasn't enough to chase Roddy from the ocean. The wind and the waves were much too important; they had shaped his identity as a person and colored his view of the world. He couldn't begin to imagine a life away from the ocean.

On March 14, 1993, Roddy and surfing buddy John Gangini were eager to take advantage of a north swell that was slamming into Maui. The big waves promised to deliver a full dose of excitement, but they were in a quandary all too familiar to surfers everywhere. They wanted to pick the spot where the waves would be breaking best, but if they made the wrong decision, they risked driving around all day and surfing nowhere.

Anxious to get in the water, they quickly checked the waves at Ho'okipa and other surf spots near Roddy's home, but the blustery trade winds had ripped the waves to shreds. Another dilemma. They could spend nearly two hours speeding to Honolua Bay on Maui's distant northwest coast, where the wind would be offshore, or they could zip along the Hāna Highway forty-five minutes to Honomanū Bay, where steep cliffs might protect the waves from the wind.

A toss of a coin sent them to Honomanū, but storm-tossed seas greeted them when they pulled up in front of the usual surf spot. Discouraged, they continued farther along the Hāna Highway to Wailua Bay, where they saw some friends surfing fair five-foot waves.

It was now three in the afternoon, and they realized this was their last chance to surf for the day.

The pair paddled out and joined their friends in the lineup, but the waves were swarming with energetic younger surfers who were more annoying than a flock of squawking mynah birds. After a half hour the crowd finally drove their friends to the beach, but the waves had scarcely whetted Roddy and John's appetite.

They had heard of a fabulous surf spot with the intriguing name of Paradise around the headland in the next bay and figured this was the best time to head over and see whether it deserved its name.

There are only two ways to reach Paradise, each with its merits. You can take the trail over the headland at full speed and reach the waves in twenty-five minutes, but everywhere are temptations to slow down and enjoy the journey. It's part of the ancient Hawaiian kings' trail, partially paved with cobblestones that weave through a bamboo forest so dense that it creates gloom even in full daylight. At every turn is a breathtaking view of the ocean or valleys. Because the trail isn't marked well, travelers often lose their way.

Paddling from bay to bay takes half the time, and the two surfers started stroking strongly for Paradise, powered by a fierce hunger for more waves.

When they rounded the headland, they stopped dead in the water in midstroke. They had truly reached paradise. Twin waterfalls cascaded through a valley filled with exotic tropical foliage. Two streams emptied into the ocean, separated by a palm-lined shore. It was the most beautiful sight either had seen in decades of surfing in Hawai'i.

And on the far side of the bay was perfect surf, rights that jacked up over a shallow ledge and pitched out in a tube that peeled to the shore. The valley funneled the howling wind straight offshore, making the waves clean and desirable. An adept surfer could speed along the wave and step off right onto the rock-covered beach.

The sight was so compelling that the two churned the water in their haste to sample the surf. They didn't pause to wonder why local surfers were standing on shore instead of riding the delectable waves.

As the waves beckoned, the two surfers hit a witches' brew of debris from the streams, branches and twigs and leaves swirling in the current. It looked like a perfect hunting ground for sharks, and the thought sparked a sixth sense in Roddy.

Suddenly, visions of the giant tiger shark filled his mind. He

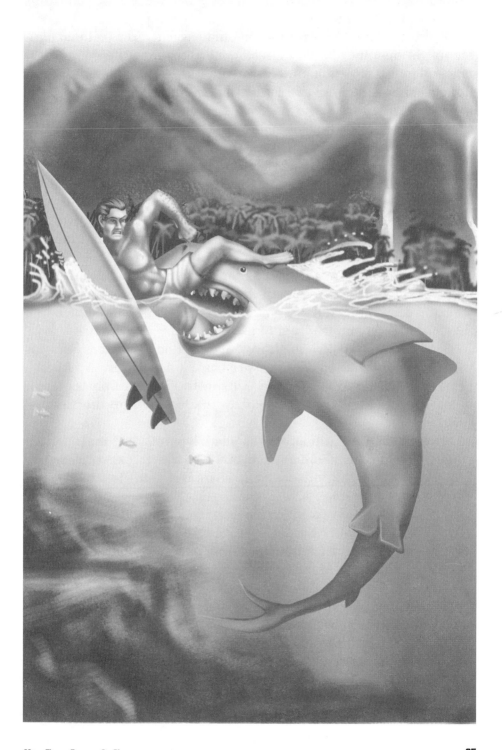

shifted into a wary mode, but his desire for the waves was so strong that he resumed plowing through the debris at top speed.

Roddy kept his eyes firmly fixed on the waves as he paddled closer, and in his mind he was already speeding along the long walls, powering off the bottom and snapping off the top. Suddenly, something slammed into him and Roddy felt an incredible pain.

An unknown force had grabbed him, and Roddy felt something tear through the meat of his right calf and hit the leg bone. He bellowed in fear and pain, and looked over his shoulder to see what in the hell had hit him.

He was horrified to find that the shadowy shark that had haunted him for so long had become reality. A tiger shark had sunk its rows of serrated teeth into him and was devouring his leg. The tiger had ambushed him from below, and with an unbearably painful hold on his leg it was trying to pull Roddy underwater.

It was every person's worst nightmare, to be eaten alive by a huge predator. Roddy dented his surfboard as he clung with maniacal strength, certain that if he let go the shark would pull him down into the murky water and tear him to pieces.

The shark struggled mightily to pull Roddy under, but was thwarted by the buoyancy of his surfboard. It moved forward to get a better grip on Roddy's leg, sinking its teeth higher up on his leg. It began shaking Roddy violently to rip the leg right off the terrified surfer.

It was a tactical blunder on the shark's part. It had moved close enough to let Roddy counterattack, and fear was quickly replaced by fury. He was only thirty-five, and no shark was going to take him out when he was so young.

The shark's head was in his lap as it worked its teeth furiously to saw his leg off, and it was close to succeeding. Roddy knew it was now or never, so he loaded his rage into one powerful blow and hit the shark on the side of the head so hard that he tore a tendon in his left fist.

The shark released its frightful grip on Roddy's mangled leg and vanished into the murky water.

John watched the drama with disbelief, certain his friend would be killed and other sharks would appear and attack any other person they could find. When he saw Roddy hammer the beast, John stroked urgently for shore, hoping that Roddy was right behind him.

In a daze created by anger, fear, adrenaline and shock, Roddy paddled wildly for shore. He didn't know whether the shark had chewed off his foot, and the suspense was unbearable. So he stopped his flight to safety long enough to look at his shredded leg, and when he saw his foot, it gave him the strength to resume paddling.

But Roddy wasn't safe yet, from the shark, or from the terrifying images in his mind's eye. He felt confident that if he made it to the beach he could survive, even though his leg was bleeding profusely. Yet it took a massive effort of will to put his arm into the water with each stroke. In his mind he could see the shark beneath him, hungry for another taste of his flesh. But he forced himself to paddle, and stroke by stroke he neared land until finally he bumped his board up against the boulders lining the shore.

He stood shakily, testing his mangled leg, and with each step a river of blood gushed down his leg and flowed into the water. Roddy survived the terror of the attack and paddle, so he was unfazed by the sight of his lower leg torn open to the bone. He had the presence of mind to take the leash from his surfboard and tie it below his knee to stop the flow of blood.

Two Wailua resident surfers, "Papaya John" McCollum and Brian Murphy, had watched the attack from shore and rushed over to assist Roddy. Papaya John ran across the headland for help, while Brian loosened the tourniquet every ten minutes to prevent tissue from being damaged by lack of blood.

Papaya John scampered breathlessly over the trail to Wailua to phone for help, but when rescuers tried to reach the wounded surfer they found that gusty winds had toppled trees, blocking the road to Wailua. They had to telephone across the island to Wailea to get a private helicopter to carry medics to Roddy.

During the ninety minutes it took for rescuers to arrive, Roddy sang praises to God and found the peace of mind to accept his possible death. But when the helicopter finally arrived and carried him to Wailua, the medics were determined to keep Roddy from his heavenly reward. His injuries stabilized, Roddy was transported to Wailuku, where doctors at Maui Memorial Hospital worked feverishly to restore his hideously injured leg.

Surgeons pulled the distinctive hooked tooth of a tiger shark from Roddy's ankle bone and later gave it to him as a memento of his brush with death.

It was the first of five surgeries needed to repair his leg. Doctors used nearly two hundred staples and numerous internal sutures to close two fourteen-inch gaping cuts on the inside and outside of his right leg and a four-inch gash on his left leg.

But Roddy felt that his worst injury was inflicted by the state Shark Task Force, which was in charge of responding after shark attacks. Task force members decided not to hunt for the shark that had attacked Roddy, saying area Hawaiians wanted the shark to be left alone.

Further, they said, the rough ocean would prevent them from setting baited hooks in the area, giving the culprit time to move to another location. And the visiting surfers should have realized that local surfers were watching the waves from shore because conditions were prime for a shark attack. The streams were discharging the runoff from recent rainstorms, creating murky water in which a shark might mistake a surfer for its natural prey. And a dead cow and pig had been washed into the ocean near where Roddy and John were surfing, which is like ringing the dinner bell for tiger sharks.

Roddy voiced his anger from his hospital bed, wondering aloud how many people needed to be eaten for the state to take action. Brian Murphy listened to Roddy's outrage sympathetically, and he left the hospital to ask fellow Wailua resident Doug Camanse to help hunt for the shark.

It was a difficult decision for Doug, a fierce-looking Hawaiian with long, black hair, a shark tattoo on his shoulder and a sinewy, muscled body that testifies to the active life he has led for fifty years.

He believes that some sharks are 'aumākua, or guardian spirits, to some Hawaiians, but he explained in his gentle voice that this shark never had been an 'aumakua, and shouldn't be protected. "Everything I do is with feeling. If the feeling was wrong, I wouldn't do it."

Doug felt strongly that catching this shark would restore the tranquillity of Paradise. He and Brian baited two hooks with cow's liver and swam out to set the line and floats near where Roddy was attacked.

The next morning they found a ten-foot tiger shark lying on the beach, tangled in the line. They cut the shark up and brought the tail to Roddy in the hospital. In return, Roddy gave them the tooth that doctors had pulled from his ankle bone, and they matched it with a broken tooth in the shark's upper jaw.

Doug killed the shark for the community, so youngsters could swim and fish and play in the water safely, just like his children did when they were young. "After we brought the shark out, the beach felt good again," Doug said. "If I did something wrong, it will come back to me."

The pair earned Roddy's respect and gratitude for taking out the shark that had attacked him so viciously. To people who scoffed that killing one shark wasn't going to make the ocean safer all across the state, Roddy responded with a story.

"One day stormy seas tossed thousands of starfish onto the beach. Later, a boy walking along the shore came upon the starfish, and tossed one back into the ocean. An old man who had been watching the deed railed at the boy, telling him he was wasting his time. There are thousands of starfish, the old man said, and you can't possibly make a difference. The boy calmly replied, 'I made a difference to that one.'"

But while the killing of the shark eased the pain in Roddy's heart, his body was in torment. "Every time I hear it called a shark bite, it doesn't begin to describe it. The pain was so intense, it's something you take with you wherever you go.

"It definitely changes the facets of your life. For two months I felt as though I was in a different plane than what we normally think of as life."

With fierce determination, Roddy worked through months of painful therapy until he was physically and mentally at ease in the ocean again. But in the back of his mind was a nagging fear that the shark had robbed him of something special. Before the attack he was a world-class speed sailor, winning some contests and placing high in others, and he had yet to prove that he could recover his championship form.

He embarked for a series of speed-sailing competitions in Europe, and learned to his dismay that his injuries had handicapped him with stiffness and a lack of flexibility. But Roddy amazed spectators, judges and his competitors by breaking several world speed records and winning several events.

Roddy is constantly training to improve on those victories, but he has a new appreciation for life that helps him deal with the inevitable disappointments in competition.

"I had a philosophical moment when I left the hospital and first started getting around on crutches. I tried to shop for food staples, and I was down, feeling sorry for myself. I was hopping around, barely able to carry things to the checkout stand.

"Then I glanced up and saw another guy on crutches. But his right pants leg was pinned up to his belt, and it was the same leg that the shark bit on me." Suddenly, an old saying ran through Roddy's mind. "I felt sorry for myself because I had no shoes, until I saw a man who had no feet."

Roddy is happy to report that life goes on. It's a lesson he learned soon after the attack. "I walked out onto the front yard and saw blue ocean like I had never seen it before and green grass greener than I had ever seen before. It was really sweet.

"You just have to be thankful and enjoy every day, every moment. Because any day could be your last day." ▲

# Shaken Up, Baby, Twist and Shout

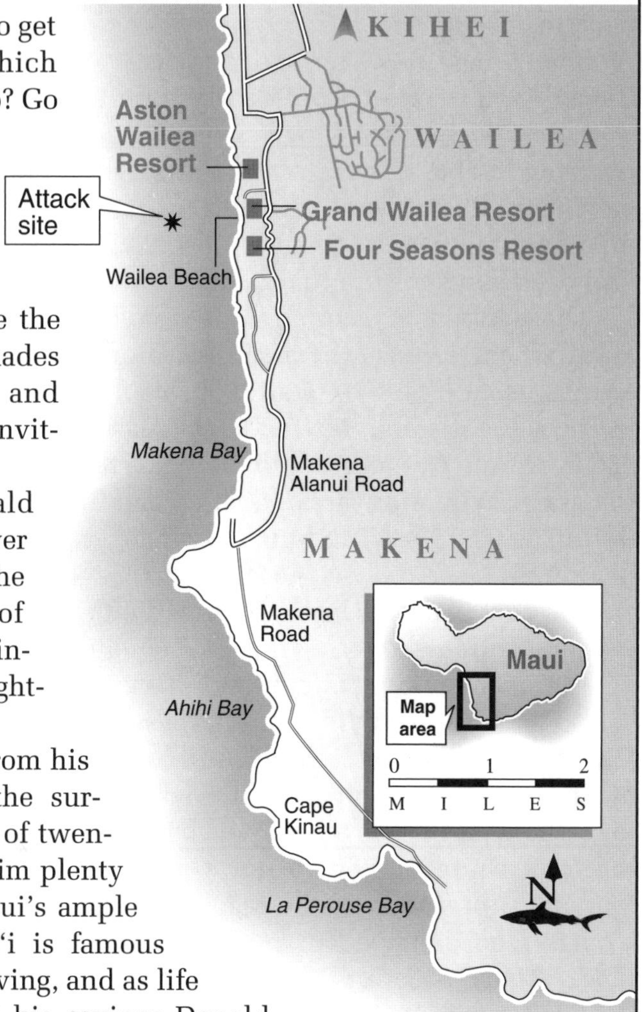

KIHEI
WAILEA
Aston Wailea Resort
Attack site
Grand Wailea Resort
Four Seasons Resort
Wailea Beach
Makena Bay
Makena Alanui Road
MAKENA
Makena Road
Maui
Map area
Ahihi Bay
0 1 2
MILES
Cape Kinau
La Perouse Bay
N


If you felt the need to get some exercise, which would you rather do? Go for a hot, sweaty run, or take a soothing swim?

What if you lived on the west side of Maui, where the ocean is a dozen shades of tropical blue and always warm and inviting? Easy choice.

That was Donald Bloom's choice, ever since he moved to the island paradise of Maui from the mainland in the early eighties.

Donald retired from his catering career at the surprisingly young age of twenty-five, which left him plenty of time to enjoy Maui's ample charms. But Hawai'i is famous for its high cost of living, and as life in paradise drained his savings Donald began to contemplate a return to the working world on Maui.

The stress and frustration of seeking a new lucrative venture built up to the point that he looked forward to his weekly workouts with the Maui Masters Swim Club, a group of men and women who shared a passion for swimming in the open ocean. Donald eagerly anticipated plunging into Maui's invigorating waters and speeding toward the horizon with swift, strong strokes.

Donald preferred to swim with other club members. The comfort of the herd helped banish anxious thoughts of the tiger sharks that certainly lurked in the depths, prowling just on the edge of his vision and, he thought, waiting for a chance to rip into his flesh with serrated teeth.

Sometimes, however, no one was available to join him, and Donald would set off confidently from the beach. But as his mind wandered during the swim, his vivid imagination sometimes dredged up unendurable images of shadows with gaping, teeth-lined jaws moving swiftly toward the solo swimmer. Suddenly, the joy was drained from his session and he would either continue in a panic or turn back and speed to the safety of shore.

Those thoughts haunted Donald much more often starting late in 1991, when tiger sharks assaulted more than a dozen surfers and swimmers, at least two fatally, during a stunning series of incidents in Hawaiian waters. But the attacks tapered off, and by 1994 there had been only two more, both off the distant island of Kaua'i, far from Donald's swimming area. Sharks had invaded Donald's thought dreams less and less, and today, Donald was thinking of nothing but pleasure.

It was a beautiful late morning, the day after Kamehameha Day, the state holiday honoring the great conquering chief Kamehameha I, who through cunning and brute force united the Hawaiian Islands.

Donald was standing on the beach on the sun-dazed coast of Wailea on Maui's southwest shore, goggles in hand and ready to give his thirty-eight-year-old body a vigorous workout. He was rarely able to recruit a partner on a weekday, but here it was Tuesday, and standing beside him in front of the Grand Wailea Resort was Margaret Maddigan, president of the Maui Masters Swim Club and a fearless woman who delighted in surfing by the light of the full Hawaiian moon. Many people went moonlight surfing once, but they abandoned it when their imagination filled the midnight-black waters with predators.

The two friends were pumped up for a swim on a familiar course that club members had churned hundreds of times: straight out from shore for several hundred yards and then parallel to shore, back and forth until their muscles ached. But today, conditions were less than ideal. The legendary Kamehameha Day swell was a whopper this year, booming into the Hawaiian Islands with the biggest south swell in twenty years.

Surfers across the state were out of their minds with excitement as they flocked to their favorite spots to ride the twelve-foot waves. But all Donald and Margaret saw was an obstacle course of murky water and big waves that threatened to choke them every time they opened their mouth to breathe.

But they weren't about to let adverse conditions turn them away from their workout. The water was refreshing as they waded into the ocean, but just as they had predicted, the usually clear water was filled with sediment churned up by the waves. As soon as they started stroking they disappeared from each other's sight into the gloom, a mere three feet apart.

The unusually large waves disrupted their strokes and forced them to swim erratically as they dodged the waves to avoid being gagged and pounded. The murky water and big waves forced the two beyond their usual route as they sought a calm area beyond the breakers, and before long they were more than three hundred yards from shore.

They never escaped the murky water, but at last they dodged the waves far enough out to find an area smooth enough to begin a serious workout. They sprinted for one hundred yards, took a brief break, then sprinted for another one hundred yards, through an exhausting succession. The cool water soothed their skin on the hot day as the sun climbed to its highest point in the sky, and they delighted in pulling themselves through the water with powerful strokes.

Donald had just finished churning the water into a maelstrom with an especially vigorous two-hundred-yard sprint angled shoreward that left him separated from Margaret by the waves. He slowly stroked over to join her, breathing hard from his exertion.

In midstroke, he felt something sharp and hard pierce his left side. "Shark!" he thought, in a flash of terrible insight. The demon of the depths had finally come to claim Donald and had him pinned in its fearsome jaws.

Instinctively, Donald launched into a maneuver he had practiced thousands of times as part of his swimming training. He rotated his body away from the pain and twisted right out of the shark's jaws. His momentum turned him so that he was out of the shark's mouth but facing his tormentor. Donald stared in alarm at a broad expanse of glistening gray flesh, and although he couldn't see the shark's head or tail, the foot-high dorsal fin told him it was a big beast.

Incredibly, after all the times he had spooked himself thinking about this moment, he was calm when the dreaded event finally occurred. Donald reared back and kicked the shark with all his might. And bounced right off the predator's immovable bulk. His futile counterattack eroded Donald's poise, replacing it with a growing fear that this fierce predator could easily overpower and devour him.

As Donald braced himself for the expected vicious attack, the shark dove into the murk and disappeared from view. Convinced that the shark was building up speed to slam into him, Donald yelled to Margaret that he had been attacked by a shark. But she needed no prompting. Margaret had seen the swirling water and commotion and immediately began swimming urgently for shore.

Donald joined her, matching her stroke for stroke, praying and fighting to stay calm and swim smoothly to keep from attracting the attention of the marauding shark or its fellow predators.

Neither remembers who won that desperate race, but although it seemed as though they were swimming through molasses, they quickly reached the shoreline and swam parallel to the rocks being battered by huge waves. Fearful that the shark was following Donald's trail of blood, they hugged the rocks while struggling to keep the waves from slamming them onto the black boulders.

When they reached the sand and scrambled ashore, Donald called out a warning to the people playing in the water fronting the hotels. Their attention was riveted by the blood dripping from the wounds on Donald's torso and left leg, and they bolted from the water.

As he gazed back out to where he was attacked, Donald spotted a few surfers waiting patiently for waves off the point. He wanted to warn them of the big shark, but he dreaded dragging his bleeding body back into the ocean. As he agonized over the moral dilemma, his fear of attack wrestling with a sense of duty toward his fellow man, Donald noticed a surfer standing on the beach, checking the waves.

The surfer's eyes widened as he listened to Donald's tale and saw his wounds. But when Donald asked him to go into the water to warn the other surfers, the young man refused. After all, there was a shark out there. Still pumped up from the attack, Donald was very persuasive, and finally the surfer paddled out to tell Donald's story to the others, watching for the shark with every stroke. They were skeptical, convinced that the new arrival was trying to trick them into leaving so he could grab all the waves for himself. Upset that he had been talked into entering shark-infested waters only to be doubted by the

people he was trying to help, the surfer became more animated as he argued with them to leave.

Finally, they all paddled in to inspect the injuries that had been described so graphically to them and were satisfied that the waves weren't worth the risk of becoming a shark burger.

As he watched the drama unfold among the surfers offshore, Donald began to ponder his good fortune. A shark that size could easily have killed and eaten him, and yet it had quickly slipped away. Maybe in the cloudy water the hunting shark thought it had captured a green sea turtle and realized its error when it bit into soft flesh and received a swift kick in the side. Maybe Donald tasted so awful that one brief sample was more than enough. Whatever the reason, he was happy to be alive.

Donald had just earned the dubious honor of being Hawai'i's first shark-attack victim of 1995 and had puncture wounds on his left leg and torso as a trophy. They formed a perfect arrangement showing how the shark had held him in its jaws, and based on the array, experts estimated that the attacker was a twelve-foot tiger shark.

Donald had rotated his torso so quickly that the shark didn't have time to take a powerful bite, and left only four punctures and scratches that Donald was able to treat himself guided by advice from his doctor over the phone.

Before his next excursion into the ocean, Donald played out the attack in his mind, marveling at his reaction and reevaluating his relationship with the ocean. "When I saw that dorsal fin, I just reacted quickly to kick it. I'm glad I did it. I must have read it in a newspaper article a long time ago.

"I realize it's the shark's ocean. Hopefully, I've learned a lesson from this. Definitely I'm not going to swim in cloudy water again. I'm going to respect their right to it. I'm not pissed off, I'm not going to say let's go hunt sharks now. Fortunately, the bite wasn't that bad. If it had taken a chunk out of me, I might feel different."

Donald has a new benchmark to add to the big moments in his life. When Kamehameha Day rolls around each year, if his mind is unwilling to recall the incident, his body throbs with the memory of what it feels like to be in the jaws of the most dangerous animal in the tropical ocean.

His self-imposed retirement is over, and Donald caters special events for the Grand Wailea Resort, right in front of his favorite swim course. Each day he can pause from his labors and gaze contemplatively out to where he was attacked.

Every Sunday he and the other members of the Maui Masters swim the same route where Donald was ambushed, although some members of the club haven't returned to the ocean since the attack. Margaret was especially traumatized by the assault, and has given up ocean swimming altogether.

For Donald, being attacked by a tiger shark has exorcised his inner demons. The attack was liberating and demonstrated to him that an attack is survivable. Donald's imagination doesn't fill the ocean with devilspawn lurking to seize him, and he realizes that a shark attack is more frightening to contemplate than to endure.

"I'm much more comfortable in the ocean than I ever was. I feel like I realize now that there are more sharks than I ever imagined, and they just leave people alone." Despite his newfound confidence, Donald increases his odds of avoiding another attack by staying away from cloudy water and swimming with friends. The whole pack of swimmers will go in the water even if it's murky, but if the water stays murky several hundred yards from shore, they will head back to the beach. After all, being attacked by mistake is just as painful as being attacked on purpose.

But the threat isn't going to keep Donald out of the ocean. "Before, I used to worry about being attacked by a shark. Now I keep my eyes open in the water, I look around me. I have an extra awareness, but I don't jump at shadows anymore.

"I feel that if I did encounter a shark I'd know what to do now—hightail it to shore. If one were to come directly up to me, I'd kick it again or hit it on the nose and let it know I'm not a turtle sitting there." ▲

# IRS Gives Blood for a Change

As Robert Rogowicz and his wife, Shirley, sped away from Maui's Kahului Airport in their rental car, Robert scarcely noticed the scenery. He didn't spare a moment to glance at majestic Haleakalā, the dormant volcano that broods over all of Maui, or gaze upon green, mysterious Puʻu Kukui, the cloud-shrouded peak of the West Maui Mountains.

Yes, yes, yes, the sugarcane fields south of Kahului were wonderful, and the views of Lānaʻi and Molokaʻi from Honoapiʻilani Highway between Māʻalaea and Lahaina were breathtaking. But Robert only had eyes for the ocean, and he was eager to swim in the waters off Nāpili that were so warm yet refreshing, even in January.

Swimming and snorkeling in those waters always invigorated him. Even though Roger treated himself to scuba diving adventures in exotic parts of the world's oceans, for decades he kept coming back to immerse himself in Hawaiʻi's soothing seas.

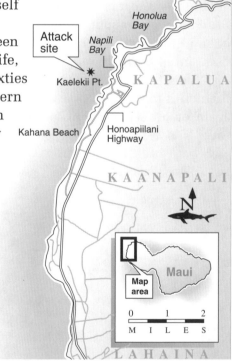

The ocean had always been an important part of Robert's life, since way back in the early sixties when he rode the Southern California surf in Manhattan Beach on heavy, thick Velzy surfboards.

He had long since traded in his surfboards for diving gear, and in the seventies he frequently joined his brother-in-law on his boat to dive for abalone in the cold, forbidding waters off Fort Bragg in Northern California.

Robert still occasionally hunted abalone with his brother-in-law, but at age fifty-three he was retired from the Internal Revenue Service, and Fort Bragg's frigid waters just couldn't compete with Hawai'i's sensuous seas.

Now he was speeding along Honoapi'ilani Highway in the early afternoon of January 16, 1996, the sunlight softly shattering into glittering diamonds as it struck the tropical blue ocean. Robert was dying to go for a swim.

He quickly checked into the Nāpili Point condominium, left Shirley to relax in their oceanfront room, and in a few quick steps was on the sandy beach holding his mask and snorkel and breathing deeply of the clean ocean air.

Back home in San Rafael his friends were being drenched by another in a seemingly endless chain of cold winter storms, and Robert was about to wade into what he considered to be the finest water in the world. He would have preferred company, but it was difficult to find someone to join him on his outings, so he was used to swimming alone.

Robert was looking forward to a vigorous swim to wash away the fatigue of his plane flight from California and hourlong drive from Kahului Airport. Even though he intended to swim fast and hard, his mask was a window to the wonders of the coral and sea life and kept him from being bored during his workout.

It was a perfect day for a swim, the water was warm and clear with visibility to sixty feet, and there was much to entertain him along his route. As he stroked about one hundred yards from shore, he spotted the usual Hawaiian butterflyfish, ornate and Christmas wrasses, a few extravagantly colorful parrotfish, and the comical *humuhumunukunukuāpua'a*, Hawai'i's state fish.

As a bonus, he saw some green sea turtles and paused to admire the effortless grace of these gentle reptiles that were so plodding when they came ashore to lay their eggs. It was almost as if the sea creatures were so happy to see Robert again that they were putting on a special show for him.

While Robert swam, he thought of all the wonderful outings he had enjoyed in Hawaiian waters. Years of diving had made Robert a realist, and he believed that as soon as he entered the water he became part of the food chain. But no creature had ever chewed on him, though he laughed to recall the time a decade ago in Kona when he reached into a hole in twenty feet of water to grab a golf ball and a moray eel clamped onto his hand.

Today all was right in the world, and Robert could feel the gentle caress of the ocean massage away his stress. He was in such a good mood that when something tugged at his feet, he calmly looked back behind him. And froze in horror.

He was staring at a huge gray animal that had his feet in its mouth. He intuitively realized it was a shark. In a reaction that outsped his thoughts, he yanked his feet from the shark's mouth, shredding his leg and foot on the rows of sharp teeth.

He didn't feel any pain; he was much too frightened. His relaxed mood was instantly replaced by panic and the certainty that he was in serious trouble far from shore.

Before he could move again, with a flick of its muscular body the shark was beside him, a creature so big and thick that Robert felt horribly vulnerable. He realized that his sure, strong swimming strokes, of which he had felt so proud, were pathetic when compared with the frighteningly powerful ease with which this huge creature moved.

While the fearsome predator eyed him at point-blank range, Robert's panicked mind called up an image of documentary filmmaker Al Giddings being menaced by great white sharks and banging them on the snout. Robert's thoughts tumbled as he searched for a way to avoid being devoured by this shark, whose tremendously thick girth indicated it would have no trouble swallowing him whole.

Robert thought that if a pop on the snout worked on great whites, aggression might chase this shark away, too. He kicked the shark with all his might, dead center in its massive torso. It was as futile as kicking a redwood tree. Desperate to avoid being attacked again, Robert lashed out with his hands and shoved the shark's thick body.

It was an equally useless gesture. The assault didn't budge the shark, but it did propel Robert away from the predator. He used that momentum to urgently flee toward the beach and safety.

Stroking frantically and breathing in rapid, short breaths, Robert was in a panic and felt as though it was taking forever to cover the one hundred yards to shore. He was convinced that the shark was right behind him, its jaws wide open and teeth gleaming terribly as it quickly moved in to finish its attack. With a massive effort of will, he looked back.

He was briefly relieved to see the shark turn and head out to sea, but he was convinced it would chase him down again, so Robert continued to churn the water in his haste to reach shore.

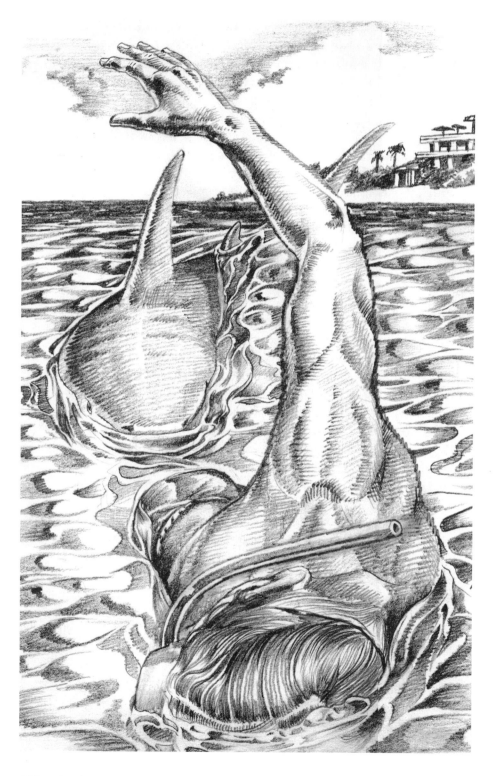

The coast south of Ka'eleki'i Point is rocky and presented a formidable barrier to Robert's escaping the water, but it was the most direct route. His wounds were leaving a trail of blood in the water, and knowing that sharks are attracted to fresh blood, Robert was desperate to reach shallow water as quickly as possible.

Once he reached shore Robert stroked parallel to the rocks until he reached the beach where he had started what was to have been a relaxing, refreshing swim. He stumbled onto the sand and collapsed as blood gushed from lacerations on his foot and leg.

Shirley was enjoying the lovely afternoon sun on the lanai when she heard Robert calling her. She hurried downstairs and was shocked to find him bleeding on the sand. Shirley was appalled by the sight of her husband's wounds and in her terror she didn't know how to handle the dreadful situation. Luckily the condo gardener arrived and sent her to the front desk to call for an ambulance while he poured hydrogen peroxide on Robert's wounds to kill any bacteria. Shirley ran upstairs and grabbed some towels to stop the bleeding until the paramedics arrived.

The ambulance ride to the West Maui Medical Center in nearby Ka'anapali was quick, and soon the doctor began the task of putting Robert back together. It took forty-seven stitches to close a gaping five-inch wound on the top of his left foot and five more to seal a cut on his right shin.

Although Robert was never able to identify the species of shark that attacked him, experts were confident that it was a tiger shark, the most deadly predator in Hawaiian waters.

Sitting in his room at Nāpili with his injured legs swathed in bandages and propped up, Robert was cheerful, laughing easily and often despite being beached by a shark attack in the first hour of his sixteen-day dream vacation.

Since his injuries prevented Robert from going for a swim, it tormented him to gaze out onto the beautiful sun-dappled ocean that drapes itself in so many inviting shades of blue. "The ocean looks so friendly, but you go out there and it can kick you around a bit," he said as a rare dark mood passed quickly, like a small cloud briefly blocking the tropical sun.

"I'm always willing to search for that silver lining. I'm eager to tell the few friends back home who might not have read the headlines about my interesting Hawaiian vacation. The good thing is that I saw a tiger shark up close and personal."

He felt lucky that the attack didn't happen back home while hunting for abalone. "An abalone diver got hit just last year near where we go diving. I have that in the back of mind when I go diving there. If it was a great white that hit me, I would have been dead."

He chuckled, anticipating the jokes about a shark getting blood from an IRS agent. His good humor is evidence that the attack will leave only faint scars on his skin and leave his spirit unmarked. Robert was eager to get back in the water as soon as the stitches are removed. Although he had never seen a shark in the previous fifty times he had swum in Nāpili and he still thinks it's a safe area, he's not going to go out in the same area again.

"I'm still going to go swimming, but I'll stick closer to shore. I knew there were sharks out here, but I didn't think one would pick on me. I knew ahead of time I would be aggressive if something happened. But you never think you'll be the one who gets hit. I've had no problems scuba diving. But it's going to be in the back of my mind when I'm swimming. I was lucky. It could have taken my whole foot off and I could have bled to death."

Robert has been scuba diving all over the world, to the Cayman Islands, Sea of Cortez and more, racking up more than three hundred dives. He eagerly anticipates a dive trip to New Guinea, and Fiji's fabled clear waters and its dazzling blue, purple and pink corals are next on his list. Sharks hold no terror for him. Once while diving in Palau at the sensational Blue Corner he was surrounded by twenty-two whitetip and blacktip sharks, and it was no problem.

Even after the tiger shark treated him so rudely, Robert and Shirley will always return to Hawai'i. No matter where else he dives in the world, Hawai'i's refreshing waters will always hold a special attraction for Robert. ▲

# You Can't Have My Board

Rick Gruzinsky was certain his life was over when his parents dragged him from New Jersey to Hawai'i in 1982. After all, how could a sixteen-year-old boy survive without his high school friends and romances?

But after a few months, Rick fell in love with the ocean, Hawai'i's most glamorous and enchanting asset. Before long he realized that his parents hadn't ended his life. They had given him a new, exciting beginning.

By the time he graduated from Kaiser High School in 1984, he was firmly hooked on Hawai'i's lifestyle. Even years spent earning a business degree in Southern California couldn't dampen Rick's ardor for Hawai'i's warm ocean and good waves. Diploma in hand, he quickly returned to Hawai'i to resume his love affair with the surf.

Actually, it was more of a harmless flirtation than a fatal attraction. Rick wasn't compelled to challenge the huge, thundering waves that produce such awe in millions of visitors to Hawai'i. Rick wasn't driven by the same inner demons that compel the hard-core thrillseekers to challenge Hawai'i's giant waves.

Rick was in it for the fun, and when the waves were

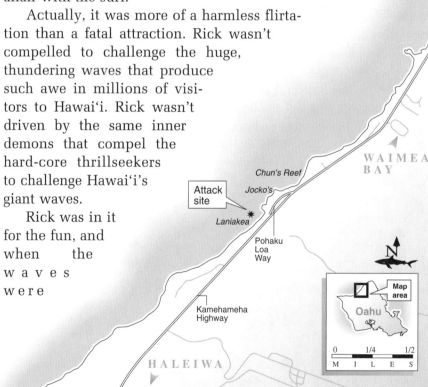

ten feet and smaller, he contrived any excuse to hit the surf. Now twenty-six, he worked with his father on construction and renovation projects, and the work left him plenty of time to surf.

As Rick cruised Oʻahu's North Shore on October 22, 1992, he wasn't thinking about sharks, even though the newspapers had been filled with accounts of tiger sharks attacking people. The year before, in the first fatal attack in thirty-two years, a woman had been partially devoured by a tiger shark while swimming just offshore of her Maui home.

And more recently, surfers had been attacked on Kauaʻi, and a bodyboarder had vanished a mile away from where Rick was checking the waves. Only his bodyboard had washed ashore, missing a chunk that fit the jaws of a captured fourteen-foot tiger shark.

Rick was preoccupied, and the thought of sharks never crossed his mind. He was busy tormenting himself with the phrase that surfers are so fond of using to bedevil each other. "You should have been here yesterday," delivered with a subtle nuance of smug satisfaction, can drive another surfer crazy.

And as Rick checked the lumpy little waves at Laniākea, one of his favorite surf spots, he sighed at the thought of his friends' tales of yesterday's overhead, glassy, peeling waves.

He had driven nearly an hour from Hawaiʻi Kai, and it was only 7:40 in the morning. The rush-hour traffic heading back into Honolulu would be hellish, so he figured he might as well get wet.

He lingered on the beach for a few minutes, engaging in a harmless fantasy that a new swell would hit the reefs as he watched in delight. He closed his eyes and pictured the waves that made Laniākea so famous.

Laniākea. The name rolled easily off the tongue, a pleasant sound that implied excitement and fun. The waves at Laniākea would hit the reef and jump skyward, pitching out in a perfect tube and peeling across the reef like a runaway freight train.

The lucky surfer could hop aboard and by coaxing all speed his surfboard could produce, would fairly fly across the 250 yards of ocean that stretched from the lava-boulder-lined point to the bridge, where the wave would taper and die in the deep channel.

Opening his eyes, Rick saw that the surf was still small and miserable. With a sigh, he paddled his six-foot-four-inch shortboard out to join a pair of surfers on longboards who were doing more sitting than surfing.

As he sat bobbing in the ocean, admiring the view of the looming Wai'anae Mountains covered in luxuriant tropical foliage, Rick hoped that a rogue set might come through and give him a taste of the great waves that his friends had enjoyed the day before.

The rogue set never materialized, and Rick had plenty of time to think about better waves. He caught a junk little wave, and as he paddled back out to the lineup, he spotted a large green sea turtle. Unfortunately, warning alarms didn't go off in his head when he saw the turtle swim away so rapidly that it created bow waves.

He caught another crummy little wave and was back out waiting for another when the ocean went completely flat. He couldn't believe that the waves could have gotten any smaller, but it was dead calm.

Rick remembers quickly dismissing an eerie feeling that arose in the back of his mind, a notion that something wasn't right.

As he paddled slowly along the lineup, waiting for another wave, he felt a roiling turbulence. No big thing, he thought, crevices in the reef frequently create boils when they release water after a wave has passed. But there hadn't been any waves, and the turbulence was getting stronger.

When he spotted a brownish green shadow under his board, Rick idly wondered why the turtle had returned to loiter under his board. Then he saw a flash of white, and something rammed his board.

Whatever had struck him was strong. It lifted the board and Rick's 170-pound body out of the water and easily rolled the board over, with Rick clinging desperately with his legs. The image burned indelibly into his mind as a large tiger shark appeared from under the water's surface and clamped onto the front of the surfboard, about a foot away from where Rick's hands were clutching the board's rails. Rick felt the impact and heard the crunch as the predator's hooked, serrated teeth chomped easily through the foam and fiberglass of his board, which moments ago had seemed so strong.

His eyes were drawn to the teeth, terrible weapons that can pin the shark's prey with sharp points while serrated edges saw through flesh and bone.

The creature was so close he could have spit in its eye, which would have been easy to accomplish, because it wasn't shielded by the opaque membrane that usually protects a shark's eyes from struggling prey when it attacks.

In a panic, Rick realized how close he was to being killed and consumed by Hawai'i's most feared ocean predator. He was clinging

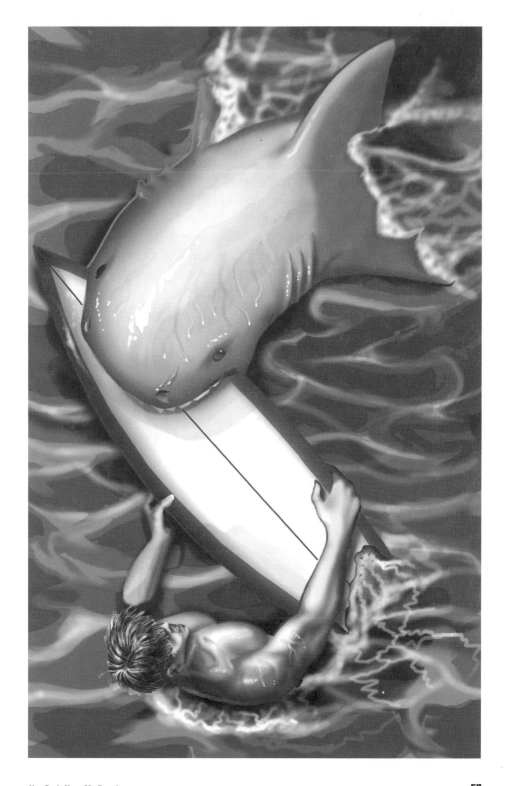

to the bottom of the surfboard, with one of its three skegs broken off and another one gouging his armpit.

Rick clung fiercely to his surfboard as the shark shook it back and forth, trying to dislodge the stubborn human. His mind told him that the shark was stronger and ultimately would pull the surfboard away and quickly devour him, but Rick wouldn't give up. His fear slowly was replaced by righteous indignation, and he became more determined than ever to fight for his life.

"I felt that was my space and my board, and I was being violated. If I had gotten bitten on the leg as a passing thing, I wouldn't have taken it so personally. But it was fighting me for my board."

So the struggle continued, until both predator and prey won a qualified victory. The shark's saw-edged teeth and powerful jaws snapped a huge chunk out of the board, leaving Rick the rest of it.

Rick realized he got the better part of the deal, as he saw the jagged fiberglass shards cutting into the shark's mouth lining as the creature tried to either swallow its prize or spit it out.

And then the shark disappeared.

As soon as his tormentor vanished, Rick attempted to set a speed record getting to shore. He was motivated by a certainty that the shark was coming back to get him and had just gone below to get a good look at its prey before pulling him under for a horrible, watery death.

Rick was so eager to escape such a grisly fate that he didn't bother to waste precious seconds turning the board over, making his escape even more difficult. He only allowed himself a quick glance to make sure his feet were still attached to his legs, and ignoring the jagged fiberglass from his mutilated board cutting into his chest, he frantically paddled the 120 yards to shore.

He yelled, splashed and generally violated every warning to make a smooth, calm, quiet escape so as not to attract the shark's attention again.

To his credit, Rick had the presence of mind to yell a warning to two surfers paddling out to the lineup. Cleverly, they took his shouted advice and sped back to shore.

Rick hit the beach a mere eight minutes later, but because every scene from every shark documentary and every sentence of every shark story flashed through his brain, the paddle seemed to take an eternity.

On shore, Rick counted his body parts and found that his only injuries were bruises and cuts from his shredded surfboard. Once news of the attack got out, government officials treated the incident as seriously as if the shark had killed Rick.

They ordered city lifeguards to close the ocean between Waimea Bay and Haleʻiwa Beach Park and scrambled a Fire Department rescue helicopter and rescue boats and lifeguards on jet skis to warn beachgoers along the North Shore of the shark attack.

It was easy to persuade surfers not to paddle out at Laniākea, because the waves were so small. But several hundred yards away at Chun's Reef the waves were much better, and the surfers politely thanked the lifeguards on jet skis for the warning and continued surfing.

The state hired a fisherman to set baited hooks just outside of Laniākea's surf line that night in hopes of hooking the culprit, just as they might capture and destroy a rogue elephant or aggressive bear on land.

Rick was on the docks at Haleʻiwa Harbor the next day when the fisherman hauled in a trio of tigers. Another fisherman came to the docks carrying a chunk of Rick's surfboard he had found floating in Mokulēiʻa, five miles west of Laniākea.

While one fisherman held open the bloody jaws of a fourteen-foot female tiger shark, the other slipped in the surfboard chunk. It fit as perfectly as a custom-made denture.

Rick couldn't force himself to touch the carcass, and he was especially unwilling to put his hands near the mouth. "I just got an eerie feeling like the thing was still alive and it was kind of like a horror movie and it was going to jump up at me," Rick explained.

"It was a sad thing to see, an animal like that dead, as big as it was. And it was scary to realize that we are sharing the ocean with things this big. I believe there is a shark problem, but I don't think shark hunts are the solution."

Four years later, Rick's life returned to normal after his narrow escape from a ghastly death. Mostly normal, that is. He still surfs at Laniākea, and he even surfs areas with a serious sharky reputation, such as the isolated coastline of Mokulēiʻa. "Talk about sharks on my mind," he says of his surf adventures.

He surfs all the time, but not alone. Never alone again. "As soon as you're out there alone, it comes right back. Don't give up the board, I always say."

He heads out to the North Shore after work and always takes time to round up somebody to surf with. "I don't like to go out in the water even if it's crowded unless I have somebody to surf with.

"I've never felt that spooky feeling, except sometimes in the evenings. My friends try not to leave me out last. If we agree on going in, I try to go in early but I always end up out there last in the dark."

There are other times he gets tingles, an intuitive warning that the sharks are hunting nearby. The places where the special feelings creep up on his subconscious are Laniākea and Leftovers, where bodyboarder Bryan Adona disappeared while bodyboarding nine months before Rick was attacked.

He wondered how he would react if he encountered another shark while surfing, and got his answer several years after he was hit. He and a buddy spotted a six-foot reef shark while they were surfing at China Walls, off O'ahu's southeast shore. The sleek shark headed straight for Rick and passed right under his surfboard, and the two friends quickly stroked for shore.

The memory of the attack has retreated to a dim, dark corner of Rick's mind and only comes forward during special occasions. After a perfect day of surfing with some friends visiting from Humboldt, California, the conversation turned to sharks.

The cold, dark ocean off Humboldt is prime hunting territory for the dreaded great white shark, and his friends were regaling Rick with tales of the heavy water they surf there. One of their friends had been attacked by a great white, and they were all still dealing with it mentally.

"I think there is something about a great white in the cold, dark water," says Rick. "Nothing could be as bad as that. The conditions here in Hawai'i are so beautiful, it's calming."

Rick joined in the spirit of the evening by recounting his attack, and brought out his surfboard and the huge chunk bitten out by the shark and passed them around.

But mostly, he is happy to let those memories remain buried. "You try not to let it paralyze you. I get in the water whenever I can. That's all I do is get in the water. That part about it goes away quickly.

"There are plenty of other things to let bother you. The last thing I want to do is worry about a fish." ▲

# A Perfect Day Ruined

Jonathan Mozo awoke before dawn and quietly slipped from bed, careful not to disturb his wife. He was eager to surf that morning and he didn't want to get involved in another emotional exchange.

His young bride just didn't understand why Jonathan would leave her and their six-month-old son Makana to go surfing with his friends. They had a happy life together, and Jonathan's business management studies at Brigham Young University-Hawai'i were going well.

If only she could feel the surge of elation that overtook him when he rode the waves, or could look around and see the beauty of the ocean that surrounded him while he waited for his next ride. And certainly the jagged green mountains never looked so lovely as when viewed from out in the ocean.

Jonathan was firmly addicted to the thrill of surfing, and no amount of tearful quarreling could keep him from the ocean.

The morning was cool and clear on June 10, 1993, with no hint of the heat that later would make everyone scamper for the shade as the sun climbed higher to beam down its fierce rays and sizzle the land.

Jonathan and his

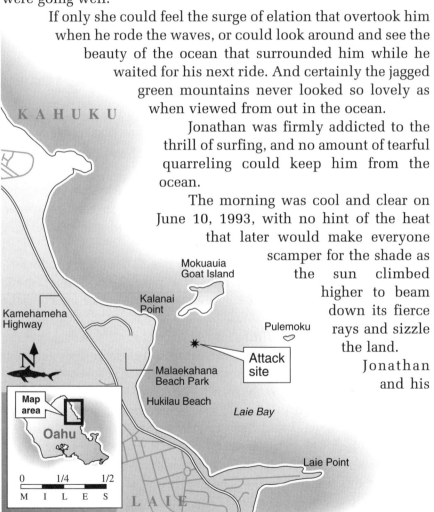

KAHUKU

Mokuauia
Goat Island

Kalanai
Point

Kamehameha
Highway

Pulemoku

Attack
site

Malaekahana
Beach Park

Hukilau Beach

Laie Bay

Laie Point

Map
area

Oahu

0        1/4        1/2

M  I  L  E  S

LAIE

best friend Ryan Bell bolted through the entrance to Mālaekahana State Park as soon as the workers opened the gate just before seven A.M. The two were keen to take advantage of the glassy, fun waves they had seen from Kamehameha Highway as they drove to the park from their homes in nearby Lāʻie.

All the kids were out of school for the summer, so Jonathan and Ryan hurried out to grab some waves before the inevitable pack of beach rats descended to assault the surf.

Their arms were powered by a sense of urgency to beat the crowd as they stroked the two hundred yards out to the lineup, Jonathan making his six-foot shortboard fly through the water and Ryan kicking hard to propel his smaller bodyboard at top speed.

They were heading for their favorite spot, called Goats after nearby Goat Island. Its official name is Mokuʻauia Island, but no one calls it that. It has been Goat Island ever since the late 1800s, when the Mormon settlers banished the ravenous beasts to the island after they ravaged the crops and gardens in Lāʻie.

The goats are long gone, and the island is now a refuge for wedge-tailed shearwater birds, a sanctuary that sometimes turns into a slaughterhouse when dogs swim from the nearby shore and savage the ground-nesting birds.

It's a surf spot intoxicating in its beauty. The waves break about one hundred yards off the lovely little island, and from the lineup you gaze out to sea at the cobalt blue deep water and waves crashing against Lāʻie Point to the south.

Looking toward shore, you see a sandy beach stretching for miles. The ironwood and coconut trees of the park hide Kamehameha Highway, while the houses of the lucky few people who live along the beach are easily visible.

Farther in the distance, fluffy cumulus clouds pile up against the sharp green peaks of the Koʻolau Mountains and drop their loads of rain to fill hidden pools from cascading waterfalls.

But Jonathan and Ryan weren't thinking about such idyllic delights as they reached the lineup and began grabbing waves. Their fear of crowds was well-founded, as surfboard shaper Jeff Johnston and his friend Ned McMahon had pulled up right behind them in the park. The newcomers watched the two buddies catch their first few waves before they too began the fifteen-minute paddle to the lineup.

Oblivious to the recent arrivals, Jonathan was having the time of his life, catching all the best waves and shredding them. "I was having a really good day, one of those days where you feel you can win any contest."

Goats was like a home to him, the most comfortable place in the world. He had surfed there more than anywhere during his twelve years of surfing, and he felt safer there than anyplace else.

Ryan was having a pretty good day, too, and was sizing up an approaching wave to decide whether he was going to catch it or get blasted by it, when he felt something bump his bodyboard.

He was momentarily alarmed, but he didn't have time to worry about what had hit his board. The advancing wave was definitely going to thump him, so he stroked swiftly and prepared to dive under the breaking wave's turbulence to escape a beating.

It was calm and quiet under the wave, and he felt a brief weightlessness that was just like flying. When he surfaced behind the wave, the peace was shattered by the horrible sound of Jonathan screaming.

The screams were blood-curdling, and although Ryan couldn't see what was going on, he was convinced that his best friend was being slaughtered.

Ryan suddenly remembered the bump he had felt.

Jonathan had been paddling back out to his friend after catching a wave when he felt a piercing pain and crushing pressure on his feet, which were hanging over the end of his shortboard. The young surfer was stunned and momentarily confused by the unexpected and agonizing sensations.

He looked back and almost passed out in terror. A huge shark had clamped down on his feet, and as Jonathan watched in horror, clutching his surfboard with all his might, the shark opened its mouth and swam forward to bite again.

Jonathan was nearly paralyzed with fear as he stared into the horrible mouth ringed with rows of sharp white teeth and deep into the beast's huge throat. It looked as though it could swallow Jonathan whole, and the grisly thought jolted him into action.

He started screaming, and jerked his legs out of the shark's mouth, tearing his flesh against the hooked, serrated teeth. Jonathan was certain that the terrible carnivore would continue to tear at him with those wicked teeth until all his limbs were shredded, then devour him at its leisure.

He continued shrieking and began paddling with superhuman speed powered by terror. He thought briefly of his wife and child and redoubled his efforts to escape.

Jonathan has no idea whether the screams scared the shark away, whether he outpaddled its pursuit, or whether the shark just didn't like they way he tasted. He never looked back as he put his head down and stroked for shore, with Ryan in hot pursuit.

His wounds were bleeding profusely, leaving a trail of blood in the water that he feared would attract his attacker and any other shark in the area. But there was a more immediate though less terrifying problem. As his furious strokes pumped blood through his body, he was in serious danger of bleeding to death.

On the beach, Ned and Jeff had seen Jonathan and Ryan catch their first few waves and began stroking out to join them. They had nearly reached the lineup when they saw the two paddling rapidly for shore. They knew something was wrong when they saw how terrible Jonathan looked, disoriented and in shock.

In a terrible voice, Jonathan told them a shark had attacked him, and they saw immediately that his feet were bleeding terribly. They quickly wrapped his urethane surfboard leash around his legs, tied him to his board to stop the bleeding, and helped him paddle to the beach.

Eight months earlier, Aaron Romento had been bodyboarding with friends forty yards from shore on the Leeward side of O'ahu when a tiger shark bit him. He bled to death in the fifteen minutes it took lifeguards to reach him, despite help from other surfers at the beach. The incident had troubled Jeff, and for months he had been thinking about what to do if he encountered a similar situation.

Jeff was determined that he was going to help Jonathan escape a similar fate. Ned was equally resolved to keep Jonathan alive and used his lifeguard emergency training to attach the makeshift tourniquet and tighten it each time the leash came unwound.

When they reached shore Jonathan was woozy from blood loss, so Jeff scampered to call for an ambulance while Ned hefted Jonathan over his shoulders and carried him the hundred yards to the parking lot.

A friend of Jeff's was just pulling up to go surfing and quickly sized up the situation. He helped wrap Jonathan's shredded feet and ankles in towels and applied pressure to stop the bleeding, then had the injured surfer raise his feet higher than his head to further slow the flow of blood.

They blazed to Kahuku Hospital in ten minutes, racing the car over the park's rough roads and nearly setting Kamehameha Highway aflame as they sped through sleepy little Kahuku town.

Jonathan's mangled feet looked so horrible that Kahuku's emergency room physician thought his tendons and muscles must surely be destroyed. He stabilized the wounds and sent Jonathan by ambulance to Queen's Hospital in Honolulu, an hour away.

It took thirty stitches in each foot to close the gaping wounds and repair a sliced tendon in his right foot, but the damage was less serious than it first appeared. Without help in the water and on the beach, though, Jonathan might never have made it to the hospital.

"If we weren't there, he would have passed out or died from loss of blood," says Jeff.

After peering down the gullet of the giant shark, Jonathan knew he had cheated death. That night as he lay recuperating in the hospital, the shark returned to him in a dream. Its mouth was gaping, its teeth were flashing, and no matter how hard he paddled, Jonathan couldn't escape.

He woke up sweating, his eyes glancing wildly around the darkened, unfamiliar room for his assailant. But the shark was gone, and never troubled his dreams again.

"I didn't have any feelings of hatred or revenge," Jonathan says. "If anything I felt grateful to him that he let me go. I felt I was out there intruding on his world, and he let me live.

"If it was our territory, we'd be born with gills and fins."

The night of the attack the state shark task force hired a fisherman to set huge baited hooks near Goat Island to catch the aggressive shark. The next day he hauled in two tiger sharks, a ten-footer and a thirteen-footer, and officials declared the hunt a success.

The news brought no comfort to Jonathan.

"That's their territory, and we're just a guest out there. The shark doesn't know any better, he's just hunting. That's all he knows."

Jeff stayed out of the surf for the next week and thought about the incident, then decided the risk of an attack wasn't worth missing waves. "If it happens, it happens. I'd rather get eaten by a shark than run over by a car."

Ryan was shaken up by the incident, but was keen for Jonathan to get better so they could resume their surf sessions.

Jonathan was even more anxious for his wounds to heal. "It was important for me to get back into the water again. I wanted to put that fear behind me. I was so happy with my life, I didn't want it to change. I didn't want to leave surfing out of my life."

Surprisingly, his wife finally realized how important surfing was to her twenty-two-year-old husband, and how his love of adventure made him the person she loved so much. Two months later, with her blessing, Jonathan paddled out at Goats for the first time since the attack.

"It kept coming back into my head, I couldn't help thinking about it. But once you get involved with surfing the waves, you forget about it," Jonathan says.

He finished his junior year at Brigham Young, then in August 1994 the little family decided to expand their horizons and see more of the world before starting a new life on the United States mainland.

They headed first for New Zealand for a month, where Jonathan sampled the cold waves south of the equator. "I got ice cream headaches from the cold water, but it was beautiful. It was a little eerie. The beaches were so barren, you could be the only surfer out for miles.

"Sometimes I would have thoughts about what was down under the surface."

They finally headed for Pennsylvania, where Jonathan's mother lives. With her help, Jonathan pursued a new passion, photography. He had decided he could learn much more about photography on the East Coast than he ever could have back in Hawai'i. But his thoughts frequently drifted back to his island home and the waves he loved so much.

"On the mainland I was dying to get in the water; it was terrible. Only a surfer knows that feeling."

Son Makana was joined by a sister, Amber, and Jonathan finally couldn't resist the lure of the islands. He had learned as much as he could on the mainland, and it was time to bring his family back to their island home and put his lessons into practice with his own studio.

Jonathan missed the ocean too much, and one of his greatest pleasures is sharing the ocean with his children.

So far, the shark attack hasn't been a problem for the kids. Amber is too young to understand, and at four, Makana has seen the video and photographs of the attack and its aftermath, and it's no big deal. "Papa got bit by a shark," he says with a gleeful squeal.

The scars aren't noticeable to the casual observer, except for one that is a source of amusement. "There is this one little thing on my ankle, it's a weird way the skin goes from the scar. I tell my son to put his finger there and I flex my foot and it pinches his finger."

Nowadays Jonathan is busy establishing his studio as a fashion photographer, and the demands of family and work keep him from the waves. But he makes time to get in the ocean when the waves are especially good. "It's a good part of my life, it keeps things in balance.

"Everyone has something like that. I feel sorry for those who don't have something as good as surfing."

The attack is way in the past, just another interesting story that he can tell to amaze strangers. "If anything, I think it happened for a good reason. It put things into perspective for me. Every cloud really does have a silver lining." ▲

# The Reluctant Hunter

The smell of gunpowder quickly overpowers the sweet scent of the ocean. The blast of the shotgun is deafening, a shocking disruption of a beautiful, sunny Hawaiian winter morning in 1995 on O'ahu's North Shore.

With each fiery roar of the shotgun, a Remington twenty-gauge Magnum load rips a chunk of flesh from the hooked shark and showers the boat's crew and passengers with blood and salt water.

More than a mile and a half toward shore across the glassy ocean, surfers are enjoying the perfect, peeling waves at the famous surf spot Laniākea, blissfully unaware of the death struggle of a fourteen-foot female tiger shark, its mouth firmly hooked and its tail hopelessly tangled in the stout fishing line. On a nearby bobbing buoy, a thirteen-foot male tiger shark is securely snagged, thrashing at the end of its fishing line.

Seven times Harold Blomfield's shotgun roars, and still the female tiger shark clings tenaciously to life. Harold doesn't hate the shark, and neither does he fear it.

It wasn't always that way. Back in the early sixties, Harold was the most talented and bold member of a small but rugged band of scuba divers who pioneered Hawai'i's black coral industry, which now generates yearly sales of more than $15 million.

Capture site

Chun's Reef

Jocko's

Laniakea

WAIMEA BAY

Kamehameha Highway

Waialua Bay

Haleiwa Boat Harbor

N

Map area

Oahu

0    1/4    1/2
M   I   L   E   S

HALEIWA

They used the old whaling town of Lahaina on Maui as their headquarters because of its prime location. The strong current that courses through the 'Au'au Channel between Maui and Lāna'i brings a constant supply of fresh, clean ocean water that helps produce the finest black coral in all of Hawai'i.

The work is demanding and exceedingly dangerous, but the lure of making up to one thousand dollars for forty pounds of the rare and beautiful black coral is irresistible.

Humans just weren't designed to descend to two hundred feet and deeper in the ocean. Nitrogen builds up in the blood, and if a diver doesn't decompress slowly as he surfaces, to give the nitrogen a chance to disperse, he can black out and drown, or suffer the hideously painful and paralyzing bends as the nitrogen gas expands in his muscles and joints.

The seductive black coral can lure even the most experienced and daring divers to their doom, such as big-wave daredevil surfer Jose Angel, who died while searching for black coral off Lahaina in 1976.

But Harold was legendary for his safe, successful diving and always brought back the best haul of black coral. So it was no surprise when a young stranger dropped his duffel bag on the floor of a Lahaina bar in the early sixties and demanded that Harold teach him how to hunt black coral.

After scrutinizing the brash young lad, Harold agreed. Timothy LeBallister was such an attentive pupil that he soon earned the nickname of Turtle and became a solid member of the tight-knit Lahaina black coral divers.

But the haunting black coral can claim even the best. Years of deep diving ages a man prematurely as many small incidents linger in the body. Turtle finally tried to break free from the lure of black coral and left Hawai'i to start a chicken farm in Oregon.

It was no use. Even thousands of miles away, Turtle heard the call of the pristine waters off Lahaina, and he could see the glistening trees of black coral. He returned, and did well for a few more years. But in 1996, Turtle sensed that he was nearing the end of his diving career. So he tried to pass on his vast knowledge to his son, Beau.

The twenty-four-year-old Beau was afflicted with the impatience of youth. He wanted to be a black coral diver now, without compiling the years of specialized training and one thousand hours of experience necessary to become a successful deep-sea diver.

A good diver gradually goes to greater depths over at least a year to adjust to the physical stress of nitrogen buildup, but Beau took it too fast. While diving with his father one day, Beau blacked out. When Turtle saw his son on the bottom, unconscious, his years of experience were overpowered by a father's love for his child.

He dove down to 250 feet and snatched his son in his arms, then sped to the surface. The nitrogen gas that filled his blood never had a chance to dissolve, and father and son died painfully.

But such a horrible death held no special terror for Harold. He loved the freedom of diving deep beneath the troubled world on the surface. At 250 feet, he entered another realm, a beautiful, peaceful world where whales and dolphins cavorted and giant *ulua* and other fish swam gracefully by.

The lure of the black coral was enough to keep Harold diving deep forever. But he also loved his undersea world, where the water filtered out the reds and yellows and left the cool colors of the spectrum to bathe everything in blue and violet until objects finally faded and vanished into gray, and then total black.

"It gives you a mellow feeling," says Harold. "It's so beautiful that you're tempted to stay down there forever." With enough nitrogen in his system, a diver can have the sensation of being drunk, and irrational ideas seem entirely plausible. Some divers have begun to shed their dive gear to swim more freely with the fishes, only to be restrained by friends.

Black-coral divers are especially susceptible to nitrogen narcosis. Sometimes while cruising through vast deserts of sand and rock known as the rolly doldrums, a diver will see an oasis of black coral in the distance. When he swims wildly up to it, he realizes with keen disappointment that his mind was playing tricks on him.

But Harold's underwater haven wasn't an entirely peaceful world. Harold had a dread of sharks greater than any fear of the bends and other hazards of diving deep. Most of the sharks Harold encountered were merely pests that he treated with caution. What he truly feared were the tiger sharks.

With their blunt snout, lifeless gray eyes and huge mouth bristling with those wicked, serrated teeth, tiger sharks are exactly what Harold figured Satan would use as his watchdogs.

The way tigers propel themselves with a sinuous side-to-side motion is especially creepy. And they are adventuresome eaters, gobbling almost anything they encounter, alive or dead. Lacking hands to complement their keen eyesight, extraordinary sense of smell, and ability to detect electrical impulses and vibrations of swimming creatures, tiger sharks explore objects with their mouth.

To a human, an exploratory bite can be as fatal as a determined attack. To make matters worse, tiger sharks are incredibly cunning hunters. They know precisely the limits of human vision underwater and will hover on the edge of visibility as they decide whether the human is a potential meal.

Tiger sharks also constantly maneuver to get into the blind spot directly behind a diver so they can approach unobserved. And they are distressingly stealthy for such a large animal.

Spearfishermen hunting for prey back to back, continuously scanning the water with extreme vigilance, often are startled when a fifteen-foot tiger shark appears suddenly beside them.

Harold was constantly approached by the six- to eight-foot juvenile tiger sharks that seemed to take a perverse pleasure in darting at him and veering away at the last second, messing around with him like a gang of teen-age punks. But he found that much like human hoodlums, if he conked the biggest one on the snout, the others would take off.

Unfortunately, that tactic doesn't work on the adult tigers. Sharks are the jet fighters of the ocean, and a full-grown tiger can go from a lazy cruise to full speed with a flick of its tail. Its body is a solid muscle that can ram a human and rupture organs, and its denticle-covered hide can scrape the skin of a person with the ruthless efficiency of eighty-grit sandpaper on a belt sander.

Its fearsome teeth and powerful jaws can saw through bones and rip deadly chunks out of creatures much tougher than soft humans. Harold preferred the slow agony of the bends to the horror of a shark attack, and continually scanned the ocean for the silhouette of his personal nightmare, a giant shark that could swallow him whole.

And then one day, in the deepest, darkest water at the bottom of the ocean, Harold's life was changed forever. Down where the life-giving sunlight has been filtered by the water, leaving only a dim memory of the comforting light, Harold was searching for an oasis of black coral at about 240 feet.

Off in the murky distance, a shadow moved. Alarmed, Harold abandoned his search for coral and devoted his full attention to the moving shape. He prayed that it was a dolphin or young whale separated from its pod. But the sinuous motion as its whole body moved in long, lazy strokes told him that his prayer was in vain.

His concentration was so intense that he forgot to breathe as the creature came slowly closer, becoming increasingly sinister as it approached. It was a shark, probably a tiger shark judging from the maddeningly confident way it was cruising, secure in the knowledge that it was a predator without peer and had nothing to fear from any other creature.

Its head moved constantly from side to side as it searched for something to eat. The beast was heading straight for Harold, and as it neared he began to get a sense of how big it was. Its gray body and off-white belly confirmed that it was a tiger shark, the biggest Harold had ever seen, at least twenty feet.

His worst nightmare was coming true, as with strong strokes of its powerful tail, the tiger shark slowly swam toward the paralyzed diver. Still holding his breath, Harold noted that the creature's huge mouth could devour him with enough room that he wouldn't even scrape against the horrible ring of teeth.

The mental image sent him into a panic. Harold began breathing in short, fast breaths as he looked around desperately for someplace to hide from this hideous demon of death and agent of destruction. Unfortunately, he was smack in the middle of the rolly doldrums, surrounded by sand without even a rock to cower behind.

Staring toward the surface, he saw the sun shining faintly, offering the mocking hope of safety. But it would be excruciating suicide to sprint for the surface from this depth. He watched in frustration as a cascade of his air bubbles danced upward, taking the path that he dared not follow.

Amazingly, a sense of calm came over Harold. There was nothing he could do to prevent the shark from eating him, and a cosmic awareness replaced his terror. He could see the scene as if from a distance, and he realized what a little speck he was in the grand scheme of things. His life seemed insignificant when weighed against the natural order of life.

Harold relaxed as he gazed in awe at the magnificent creature. Fear turned to respect as he noticed how effortlessly the mammoth shark glided through the water. Just when he expected the creature to open its huge jaws and swallow him, the shark stopped.

Dead in the water, the shark examined Harold from ten feet away, its gray eye scanning his body from head to foot, repeatedly returning to gaze into his eyes.

Like most men who wrest a hard living from the sea, Harold chooses his words carefully and uses them sparingly. But he says with conviction that at the bottom of the ocean as he looked into the eyes of what he was certain was the agent of his death, he felt a connection.

The shark observed him, he observed the shark, and he sensed that they respected each other. And the shark let Harold keep his life.

With one last long, soul-searing look, it swam slowly away, still hunting, its head moving side to side as it searched for food. And as it moved off into the distant wall of blackness, the great shark took with it all the fear Harold previously felt for sharks.

It wasn't sharks or other dangers of the deep that weaned Harold from black coral diving. It was the bottom line. When the market for black coral dried up in the late seventies, Harold moved back to O'ahu to catch crabs, lobsters and reef fish.

During a lifetime of diving and fishing in Hawai'i, Harold has found that most of the fearful people he has taken down to watch sharks swimming free in the ocean are quickly overcome by the beauty of the sight.

Harold recognizes the important role sharks play in maintaining a healthy marine ecosystem, and in appreciation he feeds them by hand.

Galapagos and tiger sharks know the sound when Harold fires up his Maui-built, twenty-four-foot boat named *Huki*. With the Jolly Roger and Hawai'i state flag snapping in the breeze, the sharks follow as he departs Hale'iwa Harbor and motors out to isolated Mokulē'ia.

The sharks swim up like a pack of tame dogs, and Harold and crew member Tash Nakamura slip them savory tidbits as they pull up their lobster and crab traps. They even have names for the sharks—Curly, with its drooping dorsal fin, the fierce Keaka, and the others.

But some days, they kill sharks, always with regret. Although Harold doesn't fear sharks, many other people do. Now that green sea turtles are protected by law, their numbers are increasing, while fish are increasingly scarce due to overfishing.

The tiger sharks are going after the more numerous prey, and because surfers, divers and turtles share the same near-shore waters, the humans encounter hunting sharks with frightening frequency.

Although humans are seldom attacked and rarely killed by sharks in Hawai'i, logic vanishes when surfers see a fifteen-foot tiger shark rip off a sea turtle's fins, toss the 250-pound creature in the air and gulp it down. Suddenly, the surfers are convinced the sharks will devour them next.

Harold's son is a professional surfer, his brother is a surfer and their friends are surfers. When enough surfers call Harold with reports of sharks chasing them from the waves, he gives up two days of fishing to set lines baited with *aku* heads in the trouble areas.

Harold figures if these calls of distress were going to the state, officials might feel pressured to instigate a full tiger shark eradication program that could throw off the ecological balance of the ocean. Tigers feed on smaller sharks, and when the state eradicated tigers in great numbers decades ago, the population of smaller sharks skyrocketed, wiped out many of the reef fish and left anglers with empty hooks.

When the surfers and divers hear that Harold has hauled a few monster tiger sharks from their favorite areas, they are comforted, believing that they are now safe, when they were actually safe all along.

The night before, Harold and Tash set their baited lines a mile from shore off the popular surf spots of Laniākea, Chun's Reef and Jocko's. It's a beautiful winter morning, the ocean is a glassy sheet, and from the boat the fishermen can hear the happy shouts of surfers riding perfect waves.

Before they came upon the hooked fourteen-foot female tiger shark, Harold and Tash hauled aboard the head of a Galapagos shark, all that remained after a larger predator dined on the captured shark.

His ears ringing from the shotgun blasts and weary of battling the still-struggling female, Harold secures her tail to the boat to let her bleed to death. The fresh bullet holes add a grisly element to the scars on her dorsal fin, souvenirs of rough mating.

Incredibly, a video cameraman who has been filming the drama insists on going in the water for close-up shots. He asks Harold if other sharks ever come around the hooked sharks, and with a wicked grin, he replies with a terse "Sometimes."

Undaunted, the cameraman recruits his friend to guard his back against intruders as he plunges into the cool, clear blue water to capture the perfect footage of the bloody carnage.

While his friend peers into the distance, staring fiercely for any hint of approaching predators, the cameraman focuses on the pathetic image of the huge female dangling helpless, blood from her shotgun wounds drifting off in the current. The blood is joined by head-sized chunks of Galapagos shark tumbling out of the tiger shark's mouth, evidence of a last meal before she was hooked.

A sense of dread overtakes the two as they slowly begin to realize that the blood, meat and shark's struggles have created a dinner bell that will summon every tiger shark for miles. The are in the middle of a huge chum bucket, and the realization gives them a burst of energy as they scramble onto the deck of the *Huki*.

Seconds after they lift their last toe out of the water, a fifteen-foot tiger shark swims up to aggressively investigate the scene, excited by the blood and meat and eager for a meal. Weak-kneed after their close call, the pair vow to never again be so stupid as they watch the new arrival bump into the boat and nibble the hooked female.

Had they delayed a few more seconds, they might be fighting for their lives. Such gruesome thoughts vanish as Harold orders everyone to quickly lash the female to the side of the boat to prevent the free shark from stealing his prize.

The *Huki* cruises through the ocean slowly, heading for Hale'iwa Harbor several miles away. Heads turn as surfers riding the waves at Hale'iwa check out Harold's catch, and a crowd gathers inside the harbor to catch a glimpse of Harold's grim cargo.

Amazingly, the shark is still alive, though no longer struggling. Harold ties the female to a pier piling until he can haul in the thirteen-foot male and trailer the two tiger sharks to the Windward O'ahu town of Lāʻie. There the Samoans and Tongans will butcher them, send some of the prized meat to their relatives in California, and savor the rest themselves.

As they carve up the sharks, they discover that the female was carrying two dozen pups, a revelation that disturbs Harold. He hates to see any ocean creature killed in vain.

No part of the adult sharks is wasted. Harold gives the teeth and skin to friends or uses them to barter for goods and services. He and Tash have sacrificed two days of fishing, in return for an occasional case of beer from surfers thankful for their newfound sense of security.

"They are beautiful animals," Harold says, gazing out to sea. "It's a shame they attack people." ▲

# Listen When the Shark Speaks

On those crisp Hawai'i mornings when the wind is calm, Alan Titchenal can hear the waves breaking as he lies in bed. If it sounds promising, he makes the quick trip from his house at the foot of Diamond Head to his favorite spot, Suicides.

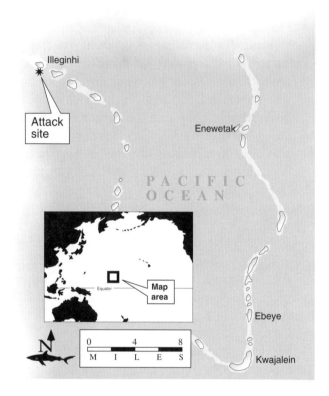

Despite the grim name, Suicides has a wonderful wave that hits the reef and peels quickly, offering an exciting ride. If you're lucky, the wave will carry you all the way to the old pier pilings sticking up from the shallow reef. If you're smart, you'll pull out of the wave before it dumps you on the pilings.

Alan loves Suicides because it's a fun wave and close to home. But mostly he loves it because Suicides is usually less crowded than the nearby surf spots beneath the Diamond Head lookout, and always has fewer surfers than the Waikīkī breaks just down the reef.

Sometimes, when he's out surfing alone, Alan casts a keen eye at the surrounding ocean, looking for shadowy shapes or the slicing dorsal fin of a shark. Although he hasn't seen many in Hawai'i, Alan knows all too well what it feels like to be caught in the jaws of an attacking shark.

Alan teaches sports nutrition at the University of Hawai'i in lovely rain-misted Mānoa Valley, just up the road from his home. But back in 1972, Alan had a more exciting if less satisfying job working for Continental Drilling, which was based in Honolulu but had projects around the world.

He rode helicopters deep into Ha'ikū and Hālawa valleys on O'ahu to do exploratory drilling for the H-3 freeway, which pierced the magnificent Ko'olau Mountains and ended up being the most expensive road in America.

Alan was excited at the prospect of a three-week contract that was to take him to the Marshall Islands, which he imagined would be wonderfully exotic. But as the helicopter flew him from Kwajalein Atoll to the job site at Illeginhi Atoll, Alan was disappointed to gaze down upon a microscopic speck of sand dotted with coconut palms. It looked as though he could walk the entire quarter-mile length of the island without even working up a sweat.

When he finally landed, it was worse than it had looked from the air. His exotic Micronesian paradise was flat as a pancake. Half the tiny atoll was a military outpost complete with top-secret missile silos and armed sentries to keep the civilians away. Alan was dejected. His tropical fantasy faded from his mind as he stood in front of his new home, an old barracks that during the day blocked any hint of cooling breeze and absorbed the sun's relentless heat with the merciless efficiency of a huge solar oven.

His only hope was that his work would leave him too exhausted to do anything but pass out quickly at night. If not, he might lie awake for hours in a pool of sweat as the barracks begrudgingly released the heat it had stored up during the day.

To preserve his sanity, Alan focused on his job. The project was simple. The government wanted to install an airstrip right on top of the reef, and Continental Drilling was to take samples to determine how much fill material was in the ocean and how much weight the reef would support.

The workers towed a drill rig on a sled along the reef and drilled at precise sites. Alan was an underwater monkey wrench boy, who sat on the platform waiting for tools to fall into the water. He then strapped on scuba gear and retrieved the tools, or slipped on a mask and fins if they had fallen into shallow water. It was stupefyingly boring work, but when he was lucky, the drill would bounce around like a Tasmanian devil and Alan would be sent down to wrestle with the bouncing drill until it bit into the reef and settled down to drill up some core samples.

The greatest danger on this tiny island was the threat of going mad from boredom. The crews could drill only at high tide, and while waiting for the tide to flood there wasn't much to do but hide from the fierce tropical sun in the barracks, playing eight-ball with crooked cue sticks on the humidity-warped pool table.

And so the ocean beckoned, promising cool relief from the sun and a world of interesting creatures to examine. Frustrated by his inability to get a decent workout walking on Illeginhi, Alan eyed an even smaller islet about a quarter of a mile away. It looked like a promising destination after a vigorous swim and offered a chance for exploration.

The only person he could talk into the adventure was a driller who had scant experience in the ocean. They set out with masks and fins and pillowcases to hold the seashells they expected to find, unaware that their first excursion was going to teach them that tropical beauty can be treacherously deceptive.

The swim over to the little island was thoroughly enjoyable, even though they didn't find the expected seashells. But as they set out on the return trip, the tide shifted, creating a current between the islands like a raging river. Alan increased his pace, looking back to make sure his friend was right behind him. As the current strengthened, Alan lowered his head and stroked like mad. Just when he felt as though he couldn't take another stroke, he reached the edge of the churning current and was able to rest in calm water.

When he looked back, his friend had vanished. Alan searched everywhere in a panic, fearing that he had lured the uncertain swimmer to his doom. Finally, he stroked to shore for a better vantage point, and still his friend was nowhere to be seen.

He sprinted to the military outpost and talked them into sending out a helicopter to search for the missing swimmer, but successive passes of the area came up empty. It was as if the ocean had swallowed him.

Alan convinced the pilots that he had a good feeling for where the current was flowing and could guide them to his friend. So Alan guided them three miles out to sea, and there was his friend. Despite his unfamiliarity with the ocean, he had inflated his pillowcase and used it to keep himself afloat while he bobbed merrily on his way to the Philippines, thousands of miles to the west.

Despite the nearly fatal misadventure, Alan and his friend continued to eagerly accept the ocean's invitation to get wet and maybe spear a few fish for dinner. It was certainly no sacrifice on their part. After all, the water was crystal clear, with no sediment or stream runoff of any sort. And the ocean was filled with a treasure-trove of coral formations and sea creatures that Alan had never seen during his many dives in Hawai'i.

He was entranced with the beauty of the fish and coral formations. Hawai'i's ocean is also a watery wonderland, but the colors in the Marshalls are much more vibrant and the sea creatures more numerous and more interesting.

The two friends would free dive, taking masks, snorkels and fins to explore the reef, and a spear gun, in case a fish was foolish enough to swim within their range. They had seen a lot of sharks, and at first the five-foot sharks were cause for alarm. Alan was young and unaware of the differences in the shark species. To him a shark was a shark, and they were all bad, an opinion shared by his friend.

Despite the anxiety the swift, sleek predators inspired, they never were a problem. The sharks would come and check the two out, say to themselves, "Oh, just some more of those weird humans," and continue patrolling the reef.

Before long, the sharks became just another interesting part of the reef scenery. After the Marshallese told them that the sharks had never bothered any of the islanders, Alan and his partner took them for granted.

Then one dazzlingly bright day they went hunting for a special type of seashell, a beautiful creature with a shell the size of a person's hand. It had graceful fingers that reached out from a center tinted orange in dramatic contrast to the creamy white body of the shell. These shells would sit on the rocks looking like hands, begging to be collected.

The friends had become so at ease with the sharks that they ventured forth on their shell-collecting expedition without spears or any other protection, only pillowcases to put the shells in.

The divers threaded their way from shore among the coral heads protruding from the water and slowly cruised about four hundred yards out, enjoying the beautiful coral and fish while keeping a sharp eye out for their prized shells.

They had snagged a few by the time they reached the shelf where the reef drops off quickly to one hundred feet deep. It was an area traditionally patrolled by the grey reef sharks.

Alan was swimming along at peace with the world, enjoying the weightless sensation of flying through the water, when he saw a beautiful shark cruising toward him. His fear of the sharks completely banished by now, Alan paused to admire how splendidly the husky six-foot grey reef shark moved through the water.

Although it was one of the bigger sharks Alan had seen, he wasn't worried. They had seen hundreds of them, and none had bothered them. Any minute it would take off and vanish into the depths.

But it didn't. It kept cruising, looking Alan in the eye and inspecting him with a keen interest that was far from comforting.

Alan's admiration for the predator began to wane as he pondered why this shark wasn't behaving like the others had, and he checked his surroundings carefully for an avenue of escape. He was in fifty feet of water, right on the edge of the drop-off. Forty feet in one direction the water was one hundred feet deep. Thirty yards the other way were coral heads he could clamber onto and escape the shark.

He was right on the edge of the shark's turf.

Alan decided to back off, to slowly head for the coral heads and give the shark some space. He moved carefully away, his eyes boring holes in the shark and his mind racing. What had he done to make this shark treat him differently?

Before he had seen the shark, he had just made a deep dive and surfaced slowly, coming straight back up. No fish swims vertically in the water unless something is wrong with it. Maybe in the shark's primitive mind it thought Alan was a sick fish, and easy prey.

Alan worked to stifle a rising panic, to keep his movements smooth and not do anything erratic that might draw any attention to himself. And he was trying desperately to seem, well, healthy. He still figured the situation was under control, but he was going to edge away and make sure it stayed under control.

Then the shark darted ahead of Alan, intercepting his path to the coral heads, and dropped down deeper in the water as Alan approached. Alan stopped and gaped in amazement as the shark did something he had never seen before. It lowered its pectoral fins, raised its snout, arched its back like an angry cat and began swimming with a rolling motion, weaving side to side and flipping its head back and forth.

It was trying to tell Alan something very important, but Alan didn't know how to interpret the body language, the only language the shark was able to speak. In fluent grey reef shark, it was saying "I'm going to attack you."

Just as Alan was thinking that he didn't like the looks of this display, quick as lightning the shark flipped a 180-degree turn and torpedoed straight for him, its teeth bared in a horrible grin.

There was no time to think. The shark was speeding straight for his heart, so Alan instinctively put out his right hand to straight-arm his attacker. The charging shark rammed Alan so hard that the impact knocked him out of the water to his waist, with the shark's jaws wrapped around his hand.

The shark used its powerful body for leverage and began tossing Alan around like a rag doll, and he went into a survival mode. His mind was going a thousand miles a minute and his body was pumped with adrenaline as he fought for his life. He was swimming as hard as he could with his free hand, kicking and thrashing and trying to let the shark know that he was alive and was going to be the hardest meal it ever caught.

But while his body was fighting fiercely, Alan's mind had doubts. Even though the shark was only six feet long, it was incredibly fast and powerful. It was as though a giant bear trap had clamped down on him and was shaking him to pieces. Alan began to think that if this shark really wanted him, he didn't have a chance.

But he wasn't about to give up.

While the shark was busy thrashing Alan's right hand, his left hand was a blur of motion as he worked desperately to reach the safety of the coral heads. Frustrated by this stubborn prey, the shark quickly changed tactics. It let go of Alan's hand and wrapped its jaws around his ribs. The pain was incredible, and Alan felt the sharp teeth grinding on his bones. The water was tinted red with his blood, and Alan began to doubt that he would survive this attack.

Alan's partner was watching in horror from twenty feet away, paralyzed with fear but unable to tear his eyes away from the grim struggle. The attack was a nightmare for the inexperienced diver, a confirmation that the ocean is a terrible place and humans have no business intruding.

Just when Alan needed help the most, his friend did the best thing possible. He panicked, and bolted for the closest coral head thirty yards away. He swam so frantically that his facemask ended up around his neck, and he was practically climbing out of the water in

his haste to escape the terrible attack.

The thrashing swimmer diverted the shark's attention from Alan, and it saw a much easier meal than the difficult creature that was putting up such a struggle. The shark left Alan and went zooming after the other human splashing through the water. Fortunately for him, he was climbing onto the coral head just as the shark reached him and barely missed biting his heel.

The shark just stopped dead in the water, floating there and taking it all in, probably thinking, "I had something. Where did it go?"

Alan was exhausted from his ordeal, breathing heavily and still painting the water with his blood. But now he had a new dilemma. He was still in deep water and an easy victim if the shark decided to attack again. And his tormentor was lurking near the coral heads that would provide sanctuary for Alan.

He had no choice. With extreme reluctance, the wounded diver cruised slowly over to the exposed coral heads, trailing blood and keeping an eye out for the shark with every painful stroke.

He finally hauled his bleeding, battered body onto the coral head and surveyed the damage, starting with his hand, which looked like custom-ground hamburger. Alan was convinced he was never going to be able to use the hand again.

The two stood atop the coral head a few minutes, watching the shark drift away and vanish from sight about fifty feet away. They were about three hundred yards from shore and tried to devise a sensible plan of action. They figured that the blood in the water might attract other sharks the longer they stood there. Both dreaded getting back into the water, certain that the shark was waiting to renew its attack as soon as Alan entered the water again.

Finally, they decided to make a break for shore before more sharks came to investigate the blood trail. They swam through a maze of coral heads in water six feet deep, looking over their shoulders and fighting to remain calm all the way to shore. The swim seemed to take forever, and when they finally reached the beach they were so relieved they could have kissed the sand.

While his friend went to notify the military guard of the attack, Alan headed to the barracks to shower. As the water washed away the blood and eased his pain a bit, Alan replayed the attack in his mind, wondering whether he could have done something more to ward off the shark. No way, he thought. "When a shark is coming at you like that, there is no such thing as hitting it. People talk about hitting it on the nose, but do that to a freight train."

By the time Alan dried off and wrapped a towel around his lacerated hand and another around his bloody ribs, a military helicopter had quickly covered the forty miles from Kwajalein. The medics put Alan on a stretcher, and he savored the rest as they flew him to Kwajalein, carried him to an ambulance and finally rolled him into the hospital.

The emergency call ended the doctor's Sunday rest, and he hurried to the hospital to dose Alan with painkillers and begin three hours of dexterous sewing to repair Alan's wounds.

The only permanent damage was a severed tendon that required follow-up surgery and left one finger unable to straighten completely. Alan is constantly reminded of the attack by a series of fascinating scars on his ribs and hand, one of which has extended his lifeline.

He also has a keen appreciation for his good luck.

"I was amazed it didn't hit more nerves and tendons. I really think I was extremely fortunate that every time the shark hit me, he hit a bony area." Perhaps genetics should be credited instead of luck, as Alan carried his 175 pounds on a six-foot-four-inch frame. The shark couldn't have hit anything but bones.

Alan didn't dive again in the Marshalls, and by the time he went back in the water again at home in Hawai'i, he was completely at ease. "I had done a lot of diving and spearfishing over the years, and in the back of my mind I always believed that I was putting myself into that ecosystem. There was always the possibility that since I was playing that game, I could become not the hunter, but the hunted.

"It was kind of like it was my turn to be tasted, and I was fortunate that I was tasted and not eaten."

Besides, Alan feels that his chances are extremely good in Hawai'i. "I saw sharks everywhere in the Marshalls, and I hardly ever see them in Hawai'i."

Although Alan has made his peace with sharks, he's more alert than he was before the attack. And if he looks for fins in the water between waves while surfing solo at Suicides, it's understandable. That's the only place he has seen a shark on O'ahu during a surf session. ▲

# Heaven Has a Bite

Rick Isbell thought he knew what paradise was. After all, he was born and raised on the Big Island of Hawai'i, the island in that lovely chain that has retained its original innocence better than any of the others.

Rick lived a youngster's fantasy, hiking in tropical forests, swimming in pools filled by cool water that sang as it tumbled over tall ledges and danced hypnotically down to the waiting pools.

He and his friends shared a generous ocean that offered fish for their spears and waves for their surfboards, and life was sweet.

And then, in 1985, Rick discovered true paradise on Tavarua, a forty-acre slice of heaven on earth just a forty-minute boat ride off the west coast of Viti Levu in Fiji.

The tiny island is surrounded by waves, perfect, uncrowded waves that offer the supreme exhilaration of long, hollow tube rides. The water is so clear that between waves Rick could gaze in wonder at coral dressed in improbable

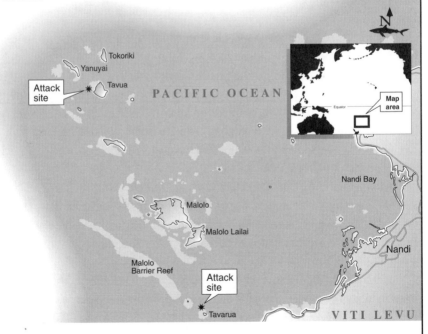

shades of purple, blue and red, and darting among the coral are reef fish more exotic than anything he had seen in Hawai'i.

Beyond the surf line, swarming flocks of swooping, diving sea birds betray bountiful schools of *ulua, pāpio, mahimahi* and tuna.

At night, the stars have no competition from manmade light, so they blaze with the cold radiance of exquisitely faceted diamonds and celebrate their supremacy in the sky by flinging shooting stars.

But the best part is the Fijians. Their size and strength are intimidating, but their every word and gesture reveals a gentle, generous temperament. Rick wanted to remain among these splendid people on their heavenly island forever, and before long he had worked out a deal with the Fijian chiefs and California surfers who controlled Tavarua.

The Californians had turned Tavarua into a surf camp that specializes in making surfers' wildest dreams come true, with perfect waves, delicious isolation, excellent fishing and an aloha that never wanes. Rick fashioned a satisfactory arrangement with the chiefs and the homesick Californians to manage the island, with help from his family and partners.

The Fijians get much-needed jobs, a lease fee for Tavarua and an additional share of the profits for their village on Viti Levu. Visiting surfers get an exceptional surf experience, and Rick gets to remain in heaven.

Before long, however, Rick discovered that a serpent infests his Garden of Eden.

It was another beautiful night in a series of beautiful tropical nights. A gentle breeze made the palm fronds murmur in their sleep, while a faint light from a slender moon twinkled across the ocean. The tide was ebbing, and across one hundred yards of reef flat, hundreds of exotic sea shells were at the edge of the reef on their nightly crawl, just waiting to be picked up.

At one in the morning, the tide was low enough for Rick and his sister Mahealani to wade across the reef and begin filling their bags with shells, which were easy to spot in the ankle-deep water. Rick heard an occasional splash coming from the deeper water, and figured it was a shark out for its nightly patrol.

With each beautiful shell they discovered, Rick and Mahealani became increasingly intent on finding more. It was as though they were in the cave of wonders and had to grab as much treasure as possible before the owner showed up to evict them. They wandered apart, each mesmerized by the hunt, until Rick heard more splashes.

He began to seriously wonder what was causing all the commotion, and decided to investigate. He shined his flashlight in the area the splashes were coming from and was alarmed to see nine sharks in a few feet of water circling the shell hunters.

One or two sharks were a nuisance, but a whole school was more dangerous than a pack of wild dogs. Rick didn't want to alarm Mahealani, who was oblivious to their peril as she happily continued gathering shells in calf-deep water. So he called out softly, "Hey Mahealani, come over here. See that little rock sticking out of the water? I want to check it out."

As the splashing grew louder and his sister reluctantly edged over in his direction, Rick called out a bit more brusquely, "Hey, come a little quicker." She continued to dawdle and the splashes increased in intensity, so Rick finally shouted, "Come over here now!"

Alarmed, she scampered over and they stepped out of the water onto the rock. Rick held her in his arms, then shined his light on the sharks, which had become increasingly bold and were darting up to the rock.

The siblings were safe for the moment and watched in morbid fascination as the pale moonlight glinted wetly off the shadowy sharks circling their haven. After an hour had passed slowly, they were dismayed to notice that the rising tide was beginning to cover their sanctuary. Although they hadn't heard any splashes for about fifteen minutes, they were reluctant to strike out for the distant shore, fearing that the sharks would attack them immediately.

The minutes crawled by and the water inched higher and higher, until it finally covered their rock. They couldn't wait any longer. The first step was the hardest, and they tensed, expecting sharp teeth to tear into their legs. The water was now waist deep, and the five- and six-foot sharks could easily swim right up to them.

It was the most agonizing walk of their lives, as they stared frantically around them while wading through water that minutes before had been swarming with sharks. The beach fairly glowed in the dark, a beacon of safety one hundred yards away that seemed to recede with each step rather than get closer.

They tried to run through the water, but the footing was treacherous, and after stumbling painfully into holes in the jagged, irregular

coral they slowed to a nerveracking walk that they were sure would give the sharks a better chance to catch them.

Finally, they set foot on dry sand and collapsed with relief, as Rick vowed never to hunt shells without a little boat to ferry him safely out to the reef's edge and back.

The misadventure taught Rick that the real serpent in paradise isn't the venomous sea snakes that crawl ashore at night, attracted by the hum of Tavarua's generators, but the bronze whaler sharks. Whenever divers in Fiji spear fish, they can expect to be visited by these sharks, eager to share the prize.

Although not as impressively large as tiger sharks and great whites, bronze whalers are feared throughout the Pacific and Indian oceans for their aggression. Also known as copper sharks because of their metallic hue, bronze whalers are members of the requiem family along with bull, hammerhead, blue, and tiger sharks, all of which have attacked and killed people.

Fiji divers have learned to dread the inevitable arrival of the bronze whalers, *Carcharhinus brachyurus*, which can reach up to nine feet in length and swarm like dogs to seize fish right off their spears. The divers battle the sharks for the fish, knowing full well that if they let them take fish once, they'll keep coming back for more.

Their persistence is legendary.

Rick took a group of guests to scuba dive off a pinnacle near Tavarua, and after only a half hour the visitors were finished for the day. Rick had seen a big school of barracuda about seventy feet down the pinnacle, so he headed below by himself to spear a few.

He shot a five-footer, which struggled mightily as he reeled in his line. He grappled to get his arm around the fish to pin it to his body and finish it off, when the barracuda squirmed off the spear and swam away.

Cursing his miserable luck, Rick watched his prey vanish from sight. He turned around and immediately had better reason to curse. There was an eight-foot bronze whaler, its pectoral fins downthrust and its back arching in a warning of attack.

The shark was intimidating as it began biting the reef like a mad dog while swimming erratically, charging toward Rick and darting away. Alarmed by the aggressive display, Rick decided the shark probably thought he was the fish the shark had sensed wriggling on the spear. Rick's heart sank as he realized he had nothing to offer the shark to keep it from attacking him.

The bronze whaler expected something to eat, and it wouldn't let Rick alone. The powerful, speedy shark charged him repeatedly, forcing Rick to fend it off with his spear tip as he headed for the surface. The boat was seventy-five yards away, and Rick kept turning circles to face the darting shark to prevent it from getting an angle at his back for a deadly attack. The swim to the boat was excruciatingly slow, as Rick kept his eyes locked on his tormentor while it charged him, then sped off in an incredible burst of speed with a flick of its tail only to charge again.

Rick was getting dizzy from turning to face the shark as it darted in at him. The creature was determined to hound him all the way to the boat, where the guest divers and boatmen watched in horror when they realized why Rick was behaving to erratically.

The boat provided no relief from the attacks. The shark was still after him, and Rick couldn't take his eyes off the shark to turn his back and climb aboard. He was certain the shark would seize the opportunity to deliver a serious, possibly fatal, bite. He continued to fend off the shark with his spear while spinning around the boat in this deadly dance with the bronze whaler.

Suddenly, the excited shark broke off from Rick and in its agitation began biting the top of the boat. It was exactly the break Rick was hoping for. He quickly flung his scuba gear into the boat and with a wild strength powered by excitement and fear, hauled himself over the side.

After gnawing the boat a little longer, the shark swam away to seek an easier meal.

As a result of years of similar encounters with sharks in Fiji, Rick has come to regard sharks with the same serenity as do most Pacific Islanders. The ocean is the islanders' playground, their larder, their source of pleasure and sustenance, and sharks aren't terrible monsters, but merely an acceptable occupational risk, the same nuisance that dogs represent to mail carriers.

To some islanders, sharks are much more. They are gods, to be revered and honored with special rituals. Since ancient times the Fijians of Taveuni Island, three hundred miles northeast of Tavarua, have believed their chiefs to be direct descendants of the shark god Dakuwaqa, a belief that continues today.

Ratu Sir Penaia Ganilau, a president of Fiji, was also a chief of

Taveuni who traced his lineage to Dakuwaqa. During his funeral flotilla in Suva Harbor in December, 1993, mourners nodded with approval when a school of sharks surfaced during the ceremonial twenty-one-gun salute and escorted the government vessel *Tovuto* out to sea, where it carried Ganilau's casket home to Taveuni Island.

Women mourners wept at the sight and proclaimed that Ganilau was a truly great chief and that the shark escort reaffirmed his blood-line to the shark god.

The worship of Dakuwaqa and reverence for sharks haven't kept Taveuni residents or visitors safe from attack, however, and there have been two fatal encounters since 1992. Despite the attacks, most Fijians consider sharks a nuisance rather than ravenous, human-eating machines.

John Jonenadaba is one of Rick's best workers at the surf camp on Tavarua Island. Visiting surfers listen seriously when John tells them the story of when he was nine years old and a shark attacked his father.

A group of ten Fijians were spearfishing for trevally and grouper from a boat near their island of Tavua, forty miles northwest of Tavarua. As soon as John's father speared a fish, an eight-foot bronze whaler rocketed toward him and clamped its jaws around his back and stomach.

The whaler shook the diver vigorously and began dragging him into deeper water. John's father threw away the fish and spear and grabbed the shark's nose and fins to force the shark to head for the surface.

Desperation to avoid a horrible death gave him superhuman strength as he wrestled the shark upward. The choice of death by drowning or loss of blood was equally grim, so he fought the shark until they broke through the surface and he was able to take a breath of sweet air.

His friends immediately killed the shark with their spears while others loaded the badly bleeding diver into the boat and wrapped their clothes around him to stop the flow of blood.

They sped off to Tavua, where they applied leaves and an herbal poultice to comfort him while they made the hourlong boat ride to the main island of Viti Levu.

They carried him to shore, wading uncomplainingly across the sharp, shallow reef that protects Viti Levu, then made the long car ride to the nearest hospital clinic. The doctor used more than one hundred stitches to sew up the bite, which tore open the skin and muscles all around his torso and left a scar that John's father was fond of showing to scare naughty children.

The attack didn't scare John away from the ocean, nor did it dissuade one of his father's brothers, who made a living entertaining tourists by feeding bronze whalers by hand in deep water.

"All the sharks want is the fish, they don't want the person," says John.

The terrible injury the shark inflicted upon his father didn't fill John with a dread of the creatures, nor did it keep him from spearfishing over the years. He enjoys working at Rick's surf camp on Tavarua Island, and although John doesn't have to fish for a living, he still loves to spearfish.

"The sharks know there is a human in the water, but they just want the fish. The sharks come sniffing around every time I dive when I spear a fish."

Usually he ignores them, but they can be tenacious. He was spearfishing right off Tavarua when he hit a good-sized trevally. On cue, an inquisitive bronze whaler appeared and tried to grab the fish right off John's spear.

Angry rather than afraid, John lifted the fish and spear out of the water. Deprived of its easy meal, the shark bit through John's wet suit, a gift from one of the island's surfer visitors, and into his torso. The shark then began chewing on the rubbery wet suit.

John was determined to keep this aggressive creature from getting his fish. The shark's teeth were doing more damage to his prized wet suit than his body, so John whacked the shark with his free hand until it let go of his wet suit. John then began swimming toward shore calmly but firmly. He wasn't moving very quickly, as he had to stroke with one arm while the other hand held his fish out of the water to protect the fish from the shark.

He wasn't far from the beach, but swimming one-handed was tedious. Whenever he dipped the hand with the fish back into the water to help out with swimming, the shark attacked again. The nasty brute followed him all the way to shore, but John won the battle of wills when he stepped onto the beach still holding his fish, while the shark swam away, still hungry.

"Every time when I see the shark, I kind of stay cool, so I know what I'm doing," John says. "Sometimes when I shoot the fish, the shark comes around and I share the fish. I give it to him, and it makes him happy.

"But sometimes when you hand the shark the fish, it learns it can get fish from people."

That night John grilled the fish and shared it with others on Tavarua for dinner, savoring the meal that tasted especially delicious because he had fought so hard to keep it. ▲

# The Dive Master's Blunder

The divers immediately had a bad feeling when they saw the bloody fish drifting out of the dive master's bait bag.

It looked as though they were headed for disaster, and all they had wanted was a nice, simple dive to admire all the exotic ocean life in the water surrounding the Society Islands.

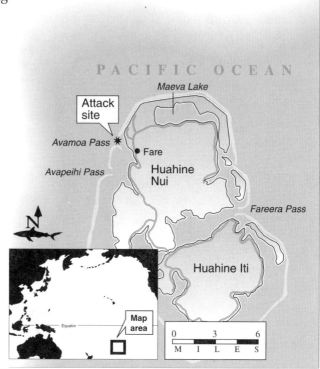

And no one was looking forward to the refreshing dive more than photographer Kathryn Bender. Her work had gone much better than she ever could have expected, and Kathryn was ready for a break. Traveling with the crews of the ancient Polynesian voyaging canoes *Hawai'iloa* and *Hōkūle'a* was exhausting, but Kathryn was satisfied that she had captured a true glimpse of the arduous but joyful life aboard those traditional vessels.

She believed that her editors at the *Honolulu Star-Bulletin* would be pleased with her photographs, and that the readers would feel they were traveling aboard the canoes among the Society Islands.

Most of the crew members of the two Hawai'i canoes had quickly fallen under the seductive spell of the South Pacific islands, which were exactly as the sailors had imagined Hawai'i must have been decades ago, before the modern world intruded so rudely.

The stars shone with cold clarity that burned holes in the dark tropical night. When the moon finally rose, it was full and fertile, whispering suggestions to young lovers. Some crew members paired off with beautiful Tahitian girls and lived out their fantasies.

By day, the turquoise waves beckoned from the outer reefs, and other crew members responded to the call, shouting with joy as they caught wave after wave and disappeared deep in the tube, only to emerge laughing.

Still other Hawai'i crewmen explored the island's beguiling lagoons and jagged emerald mountain peaks, or proudly showed off their impressive pair of ancient canoes to appreciative islanders.

But Kathryn was too tired to be seduced by the tropical romance of Tahiti; the beautiful scenery was wasted on her. All she could think about was her work, and the toughest part of the trip lay ahead.

Traditional voyaging canoes and their crews from across Polynesia had gathered in the Society Islands to perform ancient rites of forgiveness to end a curse that sundered the Polynesian nations six hundred years ago and kept them from visiting Polynesia's most sacred temple: Taputapuatea.

Taputapuatea means "sacrifices from abroad," and before the curse the elite of the Polynesian islands gathered yearly to reaffirm their ties and sacrifice humans and animals to satisfy the fierce Polynesian gods.

The ceremony was a once-in-a-lifetime chance to preserve on film ancient rites, chants, dances and songs performed by Polynesians clad in the traditional costumes of their islands. Kathryn hoped to snap classic images that would reach out to generations of viewers, and she was determined to be at her most sharp for the task.

But now she just wanted to strap on a regulator and tank and sink beneath the warm waters off the charming island of Huahine, soak away her cares and refresh herself for the difficult work ahead.

Kathryn had worked feverishly on Tahiti and Moorea to arrange a dive, but her best efforts were in vain. With increased persuasiveness, she arranged for a dive while the canoes were anchored in Huahine's lagoon, their last stop before the solemn ceremonies across the channel at Taputapuatea on the neighboring island of Raiatea.

But it looked as if even these plans were going sour. Kathryn didn't want to feed any sharks, but the dive master, a cocky young

Frenchman who had been in the Society Islands only two months, waved away her protests and those of the other divers. He was going to feed the sharks, and they had better well enjoy the show.

Gordon Damon wasn't overly excited about feeding sharks, having done it numerous times on other dives. He also was heading to Raiatea for the ceremony at Taputapuatea, only he was there for the experience, not for his job. He just wanted an interesting dive to add to the rather lengthy list of exotic dives he had made worldwide.

He also was keen to take the weight off his aching knees. Gordon moves slowly and deliberately, often aided by a cleverly designed walking stick. His knees have been ravaged by years of rugged use, but when he straps on his tanks and descends beneath the waves, he soars.

Kathryn was still steaming over the dive master's arrogant disregard for her wishes as their boat motored away from the pier at the village of Fare, but she was too eager to get in the water to confront him again and risk having him call off the dive.

Her anger turned to exasperation when the diver master began flirting with her. With an ingratiating smile and wink, he handed her the bag of bloody fish heads, insisting in a soothing tone that she be the one to feed the sharks.

When the dive master halted the boat and prepared to descend, the passengers were alarmed to see that they would be diving across the channel from a group of surfers enjoying the clean, hollow waves. They recognized many of the surfers as crew members of the two Hawaiian canoes and wondered if the dive master realized that he would be attracting sharks close to the surfers.

*Hawai'iloa* crew member Scott Sullivan was especially upset, realizing that they could be putting his friends in danger. Scott wasn't keen to go diving anyway.

As a researcher with Hawai'i-based Sea Engineering Inc., Scott had been on hundreds of interesting and productive dives, and he was in Tahiti for the grand pageantry of the gathering of the ancient canoes.

But he had become protective of Kathryn as she worked to document the event on film, and he couldn't resist when she begged him to fill the last spot in the dive party.

The dive master was in charge now, so they all followed his lead, no matter how reluctant they might be.

The plan was to dive to the bottom of the pass at about sixty to seventy-five feet and drift with the current while the boat driver followed their bubbles, ready to pick them up when they had finished their leisurely dive.

Kathryn was happy to be in the water at last, and felt all her concerns start to wash away as she savored the crystal-clear water and inspected the interesting coral formations. She recognized some of the coral, fishes and other sea life from her dives in Micronesia, but much was new to her, and she happily admired a marine environment much more exotic than anything she had seen in Hawai'i.

As soon as the first few fat, happy grey reef sharks appeared, her fury at the dive master rekindled.

Grey reef sharks, *Carcharhinus amblyrhyncho*s, usually don't find humans interesting and seldom are much of a threat. But they become keenly interested in humans holding bloody fish. They also become emboldened when a pack gathers to investigate such a scene.

When worked into a feeding frenzy by blood and fresh meat in the water, grey reef sharks can become lethal, ripping and tearing with razor-sharp teeth, twisting their sandpaper-rough bodies harshly enough to scrape a person's skin off.

They are amazingly strong, and their sleek, five-foot-long bodies move with lightning quickness and incredible agility. They will snap at each other and anything else that moves when caught up in the blood lust.

These sharks also are as territorial as a junkyard dog and will defend their patch of reef with greater tenacity than the most determined pit bull terrier, and with more deadly results.

These thoughts flashed quickly through Kathryn's mind as her fear of the sharks battled with her anger at the dive master for control of her emotions.

Kathryn's assignment was going well; she had fabulous photographs to take back to Hawai'i, possibly enough for the newspaper and an exhibition and even a book. But the ceremony at Taputapuatea was critical, and it would be disastrous if she were injured by a shark because of some inconsiderate Frenchman.

At about fifty feet the dive master opened the bag and extracted a fish head, which one of the sharks quickly snatched from his hand. Kathryn backed away from the action, unwilling to be close to the food.

More sharks gathered, until several dozen were milling around, hoping for another handout. One cruised past Kathryn, and she didn't like it one bit.

"He was looking at my legs and I knew he was thinking 'chicken, chicken, chicken for dinner.' I'm looking at him and he's looking at me, so I nudged between two divers for safety."

Gordon had returned to the boat for another weight, and when he rejoined the others he noticed that the sharks were increasingly agitated, darting here and there, circling faster and closer around the divers.

Then he saw that the dive master hadn't closed the bag after taking out the first fish head, and blood and fish were floating out. The divers were in the middle of a cloud of chum, and the sharks were becoming more and more frenzied.

They were like a pack of dogs wildly chasing after a wounded cat. Fear finally won the struggle for Kathryn's emotions, and it took all her mental strength to resist the urge to flee to the surface. She had a vivid image of the deranged sharks chasing her all the way to the boat, and winning the race.

As the circle of sharks tightened, Kathryn was certain she was doomed. "They're looking for the kill," she thought as she intently watched the scene. The dive master was busy feeding a five-foot shark when another came up underneath him. Miffed that it didn't get any fish, the excited shark grabbed hold of the dive master's unprotected right arm and hung on tight.

Kathryn screamed into her regulator. The dive master's eyes widened in alarm and pain, but he was paralyzed with surprise. Before the shark could begin shaking the diver to tear his arm to pieces, Scott quickly moved to help. He began pounding the shark on the nose, battling the creature until it let go of its prize and rocketed off to join the circling sharks.

The shark had gouged some serious chunks out of the dive master's arm, adding fresh blood to the already crimson water. Reluctantly, the dive master signaled the others to head for the boat, tacitly admitting that his shark-feeding venture was a disaster..

That was all the encouragement Kathryn needed. "I knew we were dinner, and I didn't want to be dinner," she says. The divers sped to the surface much more quickly than they should have, except for Gordon, who was older, stiffer and wiser than the others.

When she reached the surface, Kathryn rocketed into the boat as if jet-propelled, then noticed that Gordon wasn't among them. Worried that he might not have realized something was wrong and

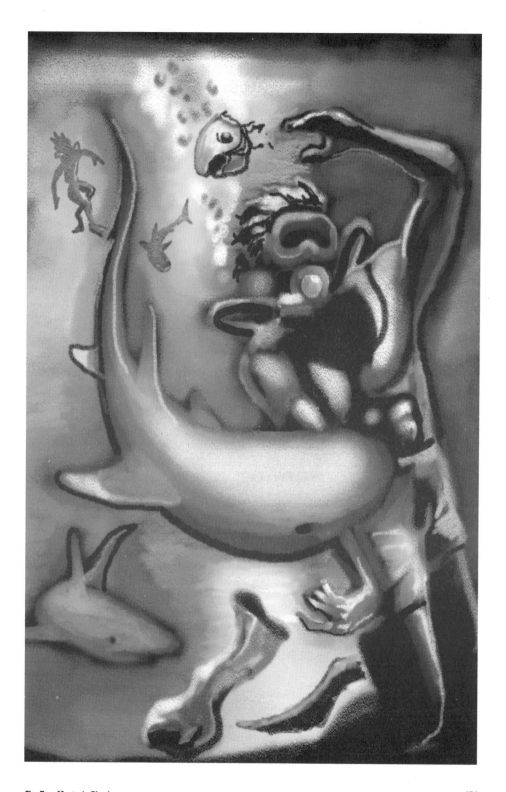

was still below in the middle of the frenzied sharks, she briefly considered going in after him.

Suddenly, he surfaced, and she reached over and grabbed him by his buoyancy compensator and hauled him into the boat.

Supercharged from the close call, she lifted the others aboard. The dive master was gushing blood from four deep cuts on the top of his forearm and a serious two-inch-square gouge off the bottom. Kathryn felt nauseous when she saw shredded meat protruding from the wound.

Blood was everywhere—on the boat, on the other divers—and Kathryn started thinking about AIDS. The dive master handed Kathryn a T-shirt to staunch the bleeding, and whether from anger at his stubbornness or excitement, she tied it so tightly that his arm turned white from lack of blood circulation.

Scott gently stepped forward and retied the arm more appropriately, and the boat sped for the dock so the injured man could be treated properly at the Fare hospital.

Kathryn was fuming the whole way back, angry to have been cheated out of the peaceful, rejuvenating dive she had worked so hard to arrange. The day was beautiful, the water was clear and she had left her cameras behind so she could escape from everything.

And they were down only four minutes.

"I was furious," she says. "But you know, when we're all sitting around telling stories of interesting dives, of all the dives I have ever done, this is the one I will talk about. My four-minute dive that was supposed to be so relaxing." ▲

# Jaws on Their Minds

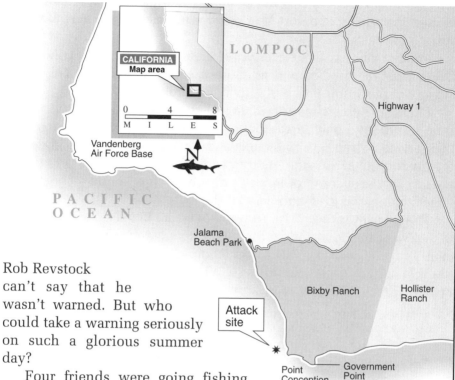

**CALIFORNIA**
Map area

0   4   8
M   I   L   E   S

LOMPOC

Highway 1

Vandenberg
Air Force Base

N

PACIFIC
OCEAN

Jalama
Beach Park

Bixby Ranch

Hollister
Ranch

Attack
site

Point
Conception

Government
Point

Rob Revstock can't say that he wasn't warned. But who could take a warning seriously on such a glorious summer day?

Four friends were going fishing and diving on a hot, sunny July 23 in 1975, and everything was perfect in the world. Rob, twenty-three, and two college buddies had allowed Rob's younger brother Scott to come on an adventure offshore of the last privately owned large chunk of wild coastline along the California coast between San Francisco and the Mexican border.

Santa Barbara was to the south, Vandenberg Air Force Base to the north, and the four boys were cruising in a sixteen-foot wooden boat off the Hollister and Bixby ranch lands, reverentially referred to as simply The Ranch by those familiar with its extravagant charms.

Only a fortunate few people had keys to the gates that helped guard the fiercely protected privacy of the ranches, which meant the waves and ocean wildlife weren't easily accessible to the hordes of people who plundered them beyond the ranch boundaries.

Rob had worked on the Bixby Ranch for a few summers during high school, and he was well acquainted with the pleasures of its off-shore waters. He delighted in riding the perfect, uncrowded waves at Razorblades, Rights and Lefts, Lefts and Rights, and Perkos, and the view of the cliffs and empty beaches was unparalleled from out in the surf.

He also had explored every promising dive area for abalone and fish and never tired of adding more exceptional experiences to his already vast accumulation of Ranch adventures.

The boys were slowly cruising in the small wooden boat north from the Bixby Ranch area, looking for the perfect place to toss out their anchor, strap on some tanks and dive for abalone or fling some fishing lines over the side. As they motored up to Government Point, the last surf spot south of Point Conception, they spotted a boat with large commercial dive numbers on the side.

They didn't want to risk running over the hookah air lines if any divers were in the water, so the youngsters carefully cruised over to chat with the commercial divers before continuing their search for the best bottom-diving conditions. When the boys politely asked the men on deck if there were any divers working below, the men exchanged sly glances and replied that no one was down there, but there was something down there. When pressed, the men replied that there was a huge shark prowling the cold depths.

Rob and his friends were immediately skeptical. There is no love lost between commercial and sport divers, who compete for the limited numbers of abalone. The boys were convinced that the commercial divers were either trying to scare them away with a bogus story or were caught up in the same hysteria that was sweeping the nation.

*Jaws* was a best-selling book and a smash hit movie, and both had succeeded in scaring people witless from coast to coast. Worse yet, author Peter Benchley had even convinced people in landlocked lakes and rivers that his demonic great white shark was lurking below, waiting for a chance to devour them alive and screaming.

Two nights earlier Rob's dive friends had cajoled him to come see *Jaws* with them, but he strongly resisted, saying he didn't want to have such bloody images in his mind when he was diving. When one friend pointed out that the chances of being attacked by a shark were more remote than being struck by lightning twice, Rob replied that those statistics are skewed by including the national population, not just the people who go in the ocean.

Scott was only fifteen and had seen *Jaws* twice. The movie had filled his mind with graphic images of gaping, tooth-studded jaws, and he didn't like what the commercial divers were saying.

Rob and his college roommate, Jeff Morris, continued to grill the divers about their shark. One diver claimed that he had been working hard to pry an abalone from a rock deep under water when he felt something tug at his fins.

Thinking it was just a seal fooling around, he kept working on the stubborn abalone. When he finally turned around to take a look, he spotted a big object swimming away. Then it made a ninety-degree turn, and he saw the horrifying profile of a great white shark at least seventeen feet long.

The diver now had the boys' full attention as he told them the shark made a few passes at him, and when he had a chance he high-tailed it up his safety line for the surface. In his panic he dropped his game bag full of abalone, and the shark quickly gobbled it in one bite.

Fearing that he was the next item on the menu, the diver fled to the boat, thankful to have lost only his abalone.

The boys were still skeptical. The diver told the story with such nonchalance that it didn't seem credible. They continued their inter- rogation, asking to see the swim fins that the shark had mauled. The diver presented them for inspection, and Rob felt his suspicions were confirmed. The fins appeared to be perfect, without blemish. Then the diver bent the blades, and revealed a series of parallel slices, as if someone had taken a single-edge razor and made parallel passes. The boys thought sure, a great white chews on these fins and that's all the damage?

The divers became impatient with the boys' doubts and said they were trying to kill the shark and weren't going diving again until they succeeded. With a gesture toward a buoy bobbing out in the bay, the commercial divers started their engines and motored their boat around the point and out of sight.

The young friends pushed off and debated among themselves what to do, but their carefree mood was quickly clouding up. Scott was the youngest, and if he had been in charge he would have gunned the boat straight for the beach, run it up on the sand for fifty yards and taken off running until his legs fell off.

*Jaws* had made a huge impression on him, filling the once-friend- ly ocean with ravenous sharks waiting to pounce the moment he set a toe in the water.

Rob and Jeff and their college buddy Tom Hesseldenz started a round of shark jokes that lightened their mood but drove Scott deeper into his paranoia.

Rob decided to cruise over to the buoy to see what the commercial divers had put on it. He slipped on a facemask and ducked his head over the side of the boat. Deep in the water was the biggest hook he had ever seen, a brutish thing of heavy metal with a huge chunk of fish stuck on it.

He whipped his head out of the water lest a prowling predator snatch him off the boat, and thought that it wasn't likely the commercial divers would go to such great lengths to scare away a few sport divers.

The friends convinced each other that the divers must have seen something large to have set that hook and that maybe today wasn't such a great day to dive. They all agreed that they would be too nervous to dive, and that it didn't make sense to take the chance.

Scott's fervent hope that they would now head for shore was dashed when the older boys decided to take a sightseeing tour to Point Conception, the great natural dividing line between Central and Southern California, and notorious for the rough waters where two major currents collided.

As they cruised, thoughts of sharks edged slowly to the back of their minds as the older boys noticed what an unusually calm day it was, with beautifully clear water that was much finer than it had been earlier. Rob, who had often surfed and dived in this area, was convinced that this was a unique opportunity for a great dive, possibly even worth risking the threat of an aggressive shark.

As they rounded the headland, they were becoming increasingly enticed by the idea of diving. They spotted some exposed rocks about five hundred feet offshore and decided to explore them. They approached the sheer rocks from the southeast, the sound of their motor masked by an onshore breeze. When they rounded the corner, they surprised a bunch of sunning seals, which reacted to the invasion by performing a spectacular group high-diving act off the rocks into the ocean.

Tom was awestruck. He grew up in Shell Beach a hundred miles north, and told the others that this looked exactly like a special spot back home that was the mother lode of abalone. He swore that they could bag their limit of abalone in twenty minutes and that they would be fools if they missed this chance.

His eloquent argument overcame their uneasiness over the lurking menace, so Rob and Tom prepared their gear to go below while Jeff and Scott readied their lines to fish from the boat.

Because he gets seasick quickly once the boat is bobbing at anchor, Rob always hustles to be the first one in the water. He quickly donned his wet suit, weight belt, tank, fins, and mask and jumped overboard.

Rob had just entered the water and was reaching for an abalone stick that Jeff handed him when he was hit by what had to be a speeding truck. Because he was slammed from below and his mask limited his vision, Rob never saw what hammered him. But he knew instinctively what had happened. After all, sharks had been the main topic of conversation and thought for the past hour. And now he was firmly in the jaws of a huge shark.

The pressure on his back and legs was intense. It didn't feel as if he was being held by an animal, more as if he was being crushed between two cars. To his horror, he could feel the shark moving side to side in a swimming motion that carried the creature straight out of the water with Rob clamped sideways in its jaws, pushing him back and forth as it wriggled.

There was a stabbing pain in his lower left leg, pierced by the daggerlike teeth of the shark's bottom jaw, while teeth of the shark's top jaw gouged Rob's upper right thigh. Both legs were being crushed by the relentless strength of the shark's jaw muscles. Just as Rob was certain he was going to die, the shark reached the apex of its leap and let Rob tumble out of its mouth.

To the others in the boat, the attack was a mind-numbing sight. Jeff was staring right at Rob when the huge beast broke the surface in a giant explosion of water, and he was horrified to see his friend clamped sideways in the shark's jaws and screaming a terrible scream.

He watched helplessly as the shark kept rising with its captive until it towered over the boat; then gravity took over and it plunged back into the ocean with another mighty splash as Rob fell free.

At the same moment, Scott saw something out of the corner of his eye. He turned quickly and stared in disbelief as his worst nightmare came true. His brother was flying through the air, screaming, in the mouth of a huge shark. It was far worse than anything he had seen in *Jaws*, and Scott was convinced they were all going to be killed. Suddenly, the sixteen-foot boat seemed much too small.

Tom had been stepping into the water on the other side of the boat when he heard the water erupt. He turned to see the shark at the height of its great leap and Rob falling from its great jaws as the massive creature plunged back into the water. The last thing Tom saw

was the shark's great tail flapping wildly back and forth, whipping the roiling water into an even greater frenzy.

Rob quickly gathered his wits and stroked like mad for the boat, fearful that the shark was gathering speed for another stunning attack. Jeff reached over the side of the boat, grabbed Rob's scuba tank and hauled him into the boat with a mighty heave as though he were a hooked bluefin tuna.

Safe for the moment in the bottom of the boat, Rob's first instinct was to count his body parts to make sure he was still as fully equipped as the day he was born. A surprisingly small amount of blood was dripping from his wet suit as Rob and his friends cautiously took inventory. They peered into a large gash in his upper right thigh, gazing dully at the layers of flesh, and although there was no blood spurting out, they recovered enough of their senses to be concerned about loss of blood.

Galvanized at the thought of Rob bleeding to death before their eyes, they tore up a white sweatshirt, stuffed pieces into the wound, and applied pressure.

Rob was in blinding pain from his left leg, which felt as though the impact had broken it in several places. They counted seven puncture wounds as they tied sweatshirt strips around each hole in the left leg, then considered their predicament. They all quickly joined Scott in his *Jaws* hysteria, convincing each other that the shark would return and destroy their small boat.

Scott sighed with relief as they began to speed recklessly to shore. Along the way, Rob tried to relieve the tension with an attempt at levity. "That shark must have thought I was just another seal in the water, and a lame one at that," he said to his humorless audience.

They took a path to the beach straight enough to please a geometry teacher and got as close as the rocky shoreline would allow. Jeff leaped out of the boat and ran off into the wilderness to try to find help.

Jeff is an extremely animated character under even the most calm circumstances, having a contagious enthusiasm for life that he expresses with great drama. After watching a great white shark nearly devour his friend, he was so pumped with excitement and adrenaline that he seemed to be flying six inches off the ground as he raced away from the boat.

After desperate minutes of searching, he came across the wife of one of the workers who were tending to offshore oil rigs. He frightened the woman out of her wits with his incoherent account of the attack, punctuated with wild gestures. She couldn't quite make out what this crazy man was saying, but she figured she had better go along with whatever he wanted or he might really get wild.

Jeff quickly commandeered her motor home and raced along the rugged ranch roads at top speed. The woman, inside the bucking motor home, tried to keep a tentative grasp on her sanity and the dishes and glasses flying out of the cupboards. After a terrifying eternity, Jeff spotted some oil workers and sprang from the motor home to accost them, leaving the woman sitting amid a pile of broken dishes.

Back on the boat, Tom pulled out his pocketknife to cut away the thick, heavy wet suit so they could take a closer look at Rob's wounds. It was a scorching hot day, and roasting in the black wet suit added to Rob's already considerable misery. Encouraged that the white sweatshirt strip hadn't turned red with blood, they gingerly pulled it away from the huge gash on Rob's right thigh.

Incredibly, the wound was bleeding only slightly, and they had a clear view all the way to his thighbone. Fascinated, they crowded around for a gruesome but interesting anatomy lesson. They carefully pulled the edges of the wound apart and scrutinized the layers of pink flesh, twitching muscle fibers and fatty tissue. It was so remarkable that they pulled out a camera to preserve the ghoulish moment forever.

This was the weird little tableau that greeted Jeff and the oil workers as they arrived to carry Rob to shore. They radioed Vandenberg Air Force Base for a helicopter to fly Rob to Lompoc Hospital, but the Air Force refused to send a chopper and instead called the hospital to have them send an ambulance to the scene.

If the shark had torn Rob up more seriously, he would have died during the hour it took the ambulance to negotiate the confusing, unpaved ranch roads to get to him at the beach.

The doctors who sewed Rob's wounds closed were clinically impressed with the high-tech cutting ability of the great white shark's serrated teeth. During the attack, the teeth were sharp enough to slice Rob's wet suit so finely that the doctors couldn't spot the perforations until they carefully scrutinized the garment. And yet the teeth were strong enough to slice Rob's thigh muscles and graze the bone.

Rob was amazed and a little chagrined to notice that slices in his wet suit were identical to those on the commercial diver's fins they had been so skeptical about.

As his wounds healed, Rob became insatiably curious about the dreaded creature that had committed such violence on him. As he talked to shark experts, Rob realized he had been as ignorant as a kitten about great white sharks.

His misconceptions about great whites came from the book *Blue Meridian*, which was made into the movie *Blue Water, White Death*. In both, the protagonist searched the world for great white sharks before finally finding one lone shark in South Australia.

That led Rob to make two potentially fatal conclusions: that great whites are extremely rare, found only in South Australia; and that they aren't native to the ocean off California. He found out the hard way that they are very native to California.

Rob always has felt lucky to escape being injured more seriously by the shark, but didn't fully appreciate just how lucky until the experts made it clear to him that the shark could easily have bitten him in half. And had the shark grabbed his legs front and back instead of side to side, it might have severed his femoral arteries and he would have bled to death in minutes, as did a diver Rob knew in Santa Barbara who died quickly after a great white bit him.

The attack on Rob didn't scar his spirit, and he immediately continued his love affair with the ocean with increased fervor. He surfed at every opportunity, bought a bigger boat and went diving more than ever. He eventually was forced to stop diving after several painful and expensive operations to remove bony growth in his inner ear stimulated by exposure to cold water. But he soon found a new love to fill the void: windsurfing.

His companions in the boat weren't so fortunate. The attack had much greater repercussions with them, because they had endured a soul-searing view of the violent assault that Rob was spared. The image has haunted Scott, who lives in the Central California coastal town of Cayucos and is very selective about where and when he goes surfing, and won't surf alone at spots that give him an eerie feeling.

Jeff was extremely apprehensive about going in the water after watching the shark carry Rob out of the water. Rob worked on him intensively, using his most persuasive tactics before getting Jeff back into the ocean, and then only on a very limited basis.

It is Rob's great regret that his daughter, eleven, and son, six, are unintentional victims of the attack. They are both reluctant to go in the water, having heard the story told over and over in lurid detail at every social function they have attended with their father.

But Rob can't get enough of the ocean. Although his family responsibilities and career as an attorney keep him out of the water much too often, he goes surfing or sailboarding even when the wind or waves aren't great, just to get in the water. He has property on the Hollister Ranch and spends a great deal of time surfing the perfect waves there, but never in the area where he was attacked.

His windsurfing takes him within sight of the rocks where it happened, and the memory is especially strong when he blows a jibe and is out there floundering in the deep water trying to right his sailboard. "I think in particular about what might be lurking down there. My mind is my worst enemy."

His mind betrays him when he's surfing at some of the Ranch's deep-water spots far from shore, such as Razorblades. When he's out surfing alone, no matter how hard he tries to think about something else, anything else, his mind keeps drifting back to stories of great white sharks, such as the one that attacked a thirty-foot boat, or the great white that rammed a kid walking out of the surf at Morro Rock in three feet of water.

Rob lives in Santa Barbara, an area that doesn't have much to attract great white sharks. The waters have been fished out and there are few protected areas where marine mammals can haul out of the water to bear their young.

But his wife is from San Francisco, and their holiday visits up north present Rob with a dilemma. He wants to surf the quality surf spots there, but surfers and windsurfers have been attacked at Davenport Landing and Waddel Creek, and a great white chased surfers out of the water at Waddel when it cruised inside the surf line close to shore.

"I don't know whether I'm going to be comfortable in either of those spots," Rob says. "It's going to depend to a large extent on how large the surf is and how bad the crowd is. If it's pumping, it's going to be irresistible."

But the attack also has made Rob savor experiences and has given him a clearer vision of what he wants out of life. "You think about how you want to spend your short time here, whether it's chasing waves and wind, or compiling money." ▲

# The Call of the Wild Places

The ocean's wildest areas have always had a special attraction for Cas Pulaski. As a student at Waialua High School in the late sixties and early seventies, Cas haunted the most isolated spots on O'ahu's famed North Shore in his search for waves.

Cas, actually Casimir, but no one ever calls him that except his grandfather who named him, was especially fond of surfing alone at Avalanche, a surf spot that has terrorized many a surfer. Avalanche is a long, lonely distance from shore and famous for huge waves that appear without warning to bury frantically paddling surfers under tons of churning white water.

Cas enjoyed the splendid solitude of surfing in such rugged places. He savored being able to enjoy the view of the island without other surfers to distract his thoughts.

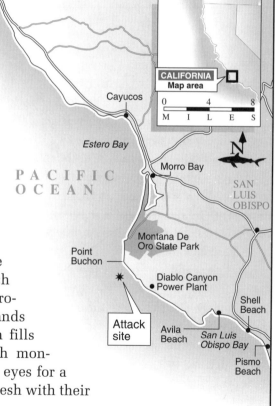

Many people peer fearfully into cobalt blue deep water and work themselves into hysteria as their mind dredges up the atavistic fears that such unfathomable water has provoked in humans for thousands of years. Their imagination fills the cold, dark depths with monsters watching with lifeless eyes for a chance to tear soft human flesh with their claws and fangs.

The ocean holds no such terror for Cas. Between waves while surfing at Avalanche, Cas liked to gaze over at the nearby Hale'iwa trench, hoping for a glimpse of the sea creatures that live in the mysterious depths. It wasn't Cas's nature to create monsters in his mind. He waited for problems to occur, then dealt with them appropriately.

Young Cas had never seen a shark while surfing, but when he and some friends were out at Silva's Channel in remote Mokulē'ia and spotted a shark cruising on a wave, they all freaked out and paddled straight to shore. Real monster, logical response, no problem.

Life was pretty sweet for a teen-ager on the North Shore, chasing waves with his friends or hunting them solo when no one else was up for an adventure. Life was pretty exciting on land, too, since Cas hung out with surfing legend Butch Van Artsdalen, who inevitably managed to provoke the biggest locals into a bar fight.

After Cas graduated from high school, he discovered the dark side of paradise. There wasn't any work, and no one was willing to pay him to surf. So in 1974 he headed for the mainland and settled in the peaceful Central California coastal town of Cayucos.

It was a sleepy little town, on the verge of quaintness. Its greatest asset was that the ocean around Cayucos was filled with just the kind of wild places Cas treasured.

He was irresistibly attracted to Malice Rock, an intimidating outcropping a mile from shore with an incredibly shallow rocky shelf that quickly drops off into spooky, deep cold water, the kind that for most people harbors fearsome beasts.

Waves from the open ocean hit the shallow shelf and pitch out into a hollow wave that is thrilling to ride if you make it. If not, the exploding wave dishes out terrible punishment, twisting a surfer's limbs into contortions they were never intended to attain.

Cas was in heaven and frequently surfed there in blissful solitude. When the waves were flat, he worked out on paddleboards to stay in shape for the inevitable return of the big waves. His favorite paddleboards were made by legendary shaper Dale Velzy, the Hawk, a friend of Cas's father since the golden era of California surfing in the fifties.

It got to the point that Cas was spending more time paddling than surfing, which complemented perfectly his job as a San Luis Obispo County lifeguard at Cayucos Pier. He would go on a water patrol during his lunch break for a welcome workout, and on weekends he would plan long-distance paddles to increase his endurance.

But his true pleasure was to let go of his thoughts through the hypnotic cadence of the strokes and see where his mind would wander. Paddling was glorious, taking Cas far from shore and providing a sanctuary from the crowds of people that were beginning to flock to the Central California coast.

The years passed in a pleasant blur of adventure-filled days. On July 24, 1982, Cas was twenty-six years old and set to begin a challenging paddle. He and friend Terry Schubert were going to spend their Saturday stroking thirteen miles from Montana de Oro State Park south to Avila Beach, just before Pismo Beach.

It was foggy and overcast, and the water was a sheet of glass at ten A.M. as they stood on the beach at Spooner's Cove. In short, a perfect day for paddling. The fog would keep them cool during their exertion, and they would slide effortlessly across the smooth water.

Cas was using a big, thick county rescue board that would make the journey easy. The county didn't exactly sanction this use of the board, but Cas reckoned that staying in shape would make him a more effective rescuer.

As the two friends waded into the water to begin paddling, they encountered a sports diver who jokingly told them to watch out for sharks. They chuckled at the diver's jest, then started stroking south. But a seed had been planted, and as they paddled, in a deep, dark corner their minds began to consider the shark the diver had alluded to.

He referred, of course, to *Carcharodon carcharias*, the great white shark, a lethally efficient result of 250 million years of evolution to create the most feared fish in the ocean. A hydrodynamically superior shape lets it speed through the water with effortless grace and economy of motion and turn its 3,500-pound body on a dime to catch smaller, quicker fish. Its jaws are lined with daggerlike serrated teeth and bite through bone and muscle with one thousand pounds of pressure to tear huge chunks of flesh out of its prey. The supreme predator's preferred tactic is to launch at its prey from below, becoming a twenty-foot missile of death that reaches terminal velocity and hits hard enough to send a five-thousand-pound elephant seal into the air. Awestruck divers have dubbed it "the white death."

Despite the hidden menace, Cas and Terry were having a great time. The paddle was as easy as they had predicted, and before long all thoughts of sharks had vanished. After an hour they were scarcely breathing hard, almost gliding across the glassy ocean. They neared

Point Buchon and were nearly within sight of the Diablo Canyon nuclear power plant, which had provoked so much resistance and protest from area residents when it was being built.

They were paddling past open country in the middle of nowhere, jealously guarded private property that formed a buffer around the power plant. Humans seldom intruded in the ocean in the area, which a state survey had determined was filled with sharks that fed on the numerous seals.

But the paddlers weren't thinking about any of that. They were a mile from shore in an area without much kelp and enjoying the rugged wilderness. They were in such a good mood that they crooned Harry Belafonte tunes.

They began singing "Come mister tally man, tally me bananas," but before Cas could get to the next line, the ocean erupted in a huge geyser of water and he was launched four feet in the air and flung from his paddleboard to land in the incredibly cold, dark water.

The impact was tremendous. As he swam to the surface, Cas was convinced that he had been slapped by the flukes of a giant hump-back whale. When he reached the surface and shook the water from his eyes, Cas wasn't prepared for what he saw. His heart nearly stopped as he watched a fifteen-foot great white shark swimming toward him.

His three-inch-thick, twelve-foot-long paddleboard jutted from the shark's mouth at a jaunty angle, like a cigar. The sight was so ludicrous that Cas almost couldn't comprehend what he was looking at. Cas froze in horror as he stared at the shark dragging his buoyant board underwater. And it was coming closer and closer.

Terry was incredulous when the shark torpedoed Cas from below and blasted him into the air. When the shark swam over Cas, Terry was convinced his friend was dead and he paddled furiously for shore without looking back, terrified that the shark would eat him next.

Cas was desperate to follow him, but swimming a mile to shore with a great white shark snapping at his legs was too terrifying to contemplate. And so was treading water while the shark mauled his board. In an incredible act of courage, Cas stroked right at the huge predator and climbed onto the tail of the board, as far from the shark's jaws as possible.

It was a huge mistake. Cas immediately started sliding down the

board straight toward the shark's mouth, which was ringed with an array of horrible teeth. He wasn't about to be gobbled without a fight, so when he slipped close enough Cas started punching the great beast. The blows were powered by sheer terror, but it was like hitting a telephone pole and made no impact on his tormentor.

Cas was staring into the shark's black eyes, and the sight shook him to the core. The eyes were dull, lifeless, devoid of any emotion or sign of intelligence, a vortex that threatened to suck the soul right out of Cas. It was the kind of thing a person sees just before he's killed and eaten.

Suddenly, the shark dropped the board and swam away. Cas scrambled onto his board and tried his best to beat Terry to shore, every stroke powered by the certainty that the shark was right behind him.

It was the fastest Cas had ever covered a mile, but it seemed to take forever. The shoreline was rocky and inhospitable, but it looked like heaven's gates to Cas as he stroked closer, resisting the tremendous urge to look back for the shark. Once he reached shore and scrambled up the rocks, he inspected his arms and legs for wounds. Incredibly, the shark had ravaged the board without harming Cas.

Terry came up and hugged him, relieved that the shark hadn't devoured Cas as he had thought. They checked out the impressive half-moon shape the shark had bitten in Cas's board and realized that the shark had come a few inches from biting off his leg.

They left the boards and trudged to the nearest farmhouse. Area residents don't get any casual visitors, and when the woman of the house saw the two wet men walking up her driveway, she suspected the worst.

"You either crashed a boat or are in some kind of trouble," she called to her unexpected guests. When Cas told her that he had been attacked by a shark, she noted the lack of blood and muttered, "Yeah, right," waiting to see where their fanciful tale might lead.

Despite her skepticism, she let Cas use her telephone to stop the person who was supposed to pick them up at Avila Beach. The woman even drove them down to pick up their boards, and as soon as she saw the evidence of the shark's savagery, she lavished sympathy on the pair of lucky survivors.

She volunteered to drive them back to Spooner's Cove, where the paddle had begun with a lighthearted warning.

It was a memorable ride for Cas. "Even though I had done that drive numerous times, everything seemed a little different that day. When you have cheated death, you respect life a little more. You notice the colors are brighter and the sounds sharper and life is sweeter."

Back in Cayucos, everyone thought that the two friends were pulling a prank with their tale of a shark attack. Then they pulled out their trump card. The shark-bitten board convinced everyone, and they were all glad the story had a happy ending.

Terry took a lot of abuse for abandoning Cas and letting him grapple with the shark alone, but Cas reckons he would have done the same thing and defies anyone to say they would have acted differently.

Unfortunately for Cas, who got a lot of mileage out of showing the board to amaze people, it was stolen. His lifeguard bosses were outraged that he had damaged county property, but the punishment amounted to a slap on the wrist. Besides, the board was already pretty beaten up before the shark took it for a ride.

One of the few reminders of the nightmare is a photo of Cas and his battered paddleboard that his sister put up in a Kailua-Kona bar on the Big Island of Hawai'i. "I've got to go visit her so I can see the picture, too," he says with a laugh, "and make sure the attack wasn't just a dream."

The attack was no laughing matter for Cas's friend Terry. It caused him to reclassify ocean paddling as a needless risk rather than relaxing recreation. He still surfs, but he only paddles for waves, and not for the dubious pleasure of roaming distant waters.

Cas, on the other hand, got right back in the water the next day and swam around Cayucos Pier. He also started paddling more seriously than ever and has competed seven times in the arduous Catalina Challenge, where competitors paddle twenty-six miles from Catalina Island to Redondo Beach in Southern California.

Cas is always training for the next Catalina Challenge, and great white sharks have yet to pay him another visit. He has seen only a few blue sharks and giant but harmless basking sharks while paddling, but he frequently gets a spooky feeling that something menacing is lurking down there.

A week after the attack he had a nightmare, similar to the falling dream everyone has where they wake up just before impact. Only Cas was being attacked by an enormous white shark and woke up just as the menacing teeth were clamping down on him.

The shark hasn't troubled his slumbers since.

Cas is troubled, however, by the changes he has seen in the central coast since 1974, when surfers were so rare they would pull over to chat when they spotted strangers with surfboards atop their cars. These days surfers are everywhere, and Cas has to go to greater lengths to find isolated surf spots.

Hordes of fishermen have scooped most of the fish from the ocean, and when Cas drops a hook and line from his board these days, it's mostly wishful thinking.

People are swarming into the ocean for all sorts of reasons at a time when protected seals and sea lions are proliferating, and the great-white population is rising as its favorite food increases in number. Cas sees humans and great white sharks speeding toward each other on a collision course, but optimist that he is, Cas believes his chances of being attacked are nil.

Still, as Cas explores for isolated new surf spots towing a surfboard behind his kayak in an attempt to maintain his treasured sense of solitude, he can't help thinking about what it feels like to be attacked by a creature that every animal in the ocean fears. ▲

# They Can't Keep a Good Man from Going Down

Map labels:
- Highway 1
- Attack site #2
- Jenner
- Russian Gulch Beach
- Russian River
- CALIFORNIA Map area
- 0 4 8 MILES
- SANTA ROSA
- Highway 1
- Bodega Bay
- Attack site #1
- Tomales Bay
- PACIFIC OCEAN
- SAN FRANCISCO
- Drakes Bay

Rod Orr doesn't mind one little bit when work is slow. The Santa Rosa, California, electrician uses the welcome opportunity to indulge in his passion for the ocean.

Over the years the ocean has given Rod generous amounts of pleasure and pain, and each of those emotions has bonded him more strongly to the sea. Some of his happiest moments have been spent in the Pacific Ocean's liquid embrace. But the ocean also claimed his father, whose body was never found after a boating accident, and is the final resting place for his mother's ashes.

Rod is suffused with strength, vitality and life when he's in the ocean, and he uses every excuse to immerse himself in its revitalizing water. The only time he turns his back on the sea is when fierce winter storms slam into the Northern California coast, their shrieking winds creating huge waves that churn the water and claw their way up the cliffs in explosions of white water.

Even the ocean's fiercest predators can't keep Rod from hunting for fish and abalone. It takes a special kind of person to go deep into the cold, dark ocean in Northern California and seek abalone in the Red Triangle hunting grounds of the feared great white shark, whose explosive surprise attacks and two-inch serrated teeth have earned it the nickname "white death."

When abalone are wedged into the rocks, a diver must pry out the shell, exposing his back to prowling predators. But it's well worth the hazards to obtain the tough meat, nestled in its rainbow-hued shell and succulent when pounded and perfectly prepared. As abalone becomes increasingly rare, it commands a huge price at the market, making more people willing to risk their lives harvesting it.

When Rod was a young and foolish twenty-year-old, he would dive anywhere, anytime, without regard for the circumstances. In May of 1961, he was hunting abalone in Tomales Bay, an area that swarmed with seals, one of the prime menu choices for great white sharks.

Rod was on the bottom of the bay in twenty feet of water working hard to pry a tantalizingly large abalone from a rock. He glanced up from his labor to see the indistinct form of a fish about thirty-five feet away at the edge of visibility. The shape was vague and set off no alarms in Rod's mind, so he turned his full attention back to the stubborn abalone and redoubled his efforts to work it loose.

As he struggled, Rod thought about the large gills he had glimpsed on the barely visible animal. Suddenly, the abalone didn't seem so important. He said to himself, "Wow, that's a shark," and looked up for a terrifying view of a young great white shark speeding toward him, its distended jaws bristling with hideous teeth.

There was no time to be scared. Rod's survival instincts kicked in, and he raced the shark to a sheltering rock. It was no contest. The shark beat him easily, and Rod only had time to raise his arm to deflect the gaping jaws downward from his chest.

The shark clamped its powerful jaws onto Rod's left hip, and as he looked down everything seemed to move in slow motion. He thought his body made a perfect fit with the shark's jaws, as though he was just an extension of the shark's head.

Fortunately, Rod's straight-arm had pushed the shark down to where it got a great bite of his weight belt and wet suit instead of vital organs. Rod feared that the shark would get frustrated with chewing on his belt and go after his arms and legs, so he grabbed its head with both hands and gouged one of its eyes with his fingers. The predator released its grip on Rod's hip, and he bolted to safety at top speed.

Rod broke the surface, grabbed his inner tube and yelled those magic words that rivet people's attention, "There's a shark after me."

His dive boat was one hundred yards away, so after calling out to his friend Fred aboard the boat, Rod stroked toward a couple fishing for halibut from a boat seventy yards closer. The shark wasn't about to let Rod get away so easily. As Rod paddled like mad for the nearest boat, the shark circled him slowly, methodically, waiting for a chance to attack again. Rod was devastated to hear the woman in the boat scream, "It's a shark, it's going to eat him!"

Determined to prove her wrong, Rod paddled and kicked even faster as the shark charged. Just in time, Fred came racing over in their dive boat and threw Rod a line. Fred was pumped with excitement and hauled Rod aboard with such enthusiasm that he cleared the side and slammed face first into the boat's deck.

Dazed but happy to have survived his first face-to-face encounter with a great white shark, Rod headed for the boat's rail to search for his tormentor. He watched in fascination as the shark surfaced, inspected the boat, then swam away.

Rod then took stock of the damage, and as he examined his cuts, torn wet suit and tooth-dented weights, he soberly considered that he might have been killed if the shark had bitten him above his weight belt.

Despite the lack of serious injury, Rod was shaken by the attack. But he figured that the trauma might be worsened by staying out of the water. Within the hour he taped up his damaged wet suit, steeled his nerves and went back into the shark-haunted water to confront his fears.

Somehow, things were different. The ocean had been his second home, and he had been completely at ease in the water. On his second dive, he was spooked when the seals came up to him.

Anyone who spends a lot of time in the ocean realizes there are many sharks out there and mentally prepares himself for an attack. But after he was hit, Rod thought he was charmed. To keep his mind from freezing in fear during the inevitable encounters with sharks, he chanted as his protective mantra, "Nobody has been hit twice, nobody has been hit twice."

The mantra seemed to protect him during numerous encounters over the decades. Rod was knee-paddling on his dive board just below Stewart's Point at the north end of Sonoma County when he heard a noise and thought, "What in the hell is that?" The answer came much too quickly. Rod spotted a dorsal fin ten feet behind his board. Then the huge conical snout of a great white shark came up beside him.

Rod looked desperately for shelter, but saw with dismay that the closest rocks were 120 yards away. He took two strong strokes, but with a lazy flick of its tail the shark was beside him, so close that he could have reached out and grabbed its dorsal fin. Instead, he stabbed the enormous creature's back with his paddle. It was as useless as poking a slab of concrete. The shark didn't even flinch, although the impact was forceful enough to bend the aluminum paddle and leave a foot-long bow in it.

Rod attacked again, this time using the paddle to shove the shark away from his board. Convinced that the shark was going to overturn his board and devour him, Rod stroked for shore like a madman until he felt soft, safe sand under his board.

Another time, Rod was part of a spearfishing competition offshore near Santa Cruz. One of his teammates was under a ledge waiting to ambush fish when a shark swam past him. He came up yelling that he had just seen a great white and told everyone to climb onto their boards. The divers didn't need much prodding as they churned the water with desperate strokes to reach their boards.

Rod spotted the shark right behind him and began swimming fervently toward his board. The eighteen-foot great white cruised ten feet under Rod, who fairly leaped onto his board. The encounter ruined the day for the competitors.

As the incidents accumulated, Rod began to wonder how many times sharks saw the divers without being seen themselves, but it was a question he really didn't want answered.

Rod was hunting underwater again when a twelve-foot great white shark made his heart beat like a drum roll by swimming at him head-on. Rod froze, then bolted for the surface. When the shark passed underneath him, Rod swam upward even faster and flew onto his twelve-foot paddleboard.

Panting from exertion, he told his diving partner he had just seen a big shark, and the guy looked at his little air mattress and begged Rod to let him on the board. Rod refused, explaining that the board would tip over. So they set out in a small, speedy convoy for the beach.

Despite the charmed life he was leading, Rod knew the ocean provides no guarantees of safety to anyone who enters. His father worked hard to wrest a living from the ocean as a commercial fisherman. In October, 1973, he was fishing twenty-five miles from the Farallon Islands when a boat fishing nearby ran into trouble.

Rod's seventy-four-year-old father tried to help solve the problem, but as darkness approached he began towing the disabled forty-six-foot boat with his own thirty-one-footer. A storm roared in, and the chaotic seas tossed his dad's boat onto the other boat, and it went down. His dad was never found, and the other boat was discovered five days later ninety miles southeast of Santa Cruz, its owner still aboard with broken ribs and a dislocated shoulder.

The incident never turned Rod away from the ocean; it merely reinforced his belief that although the ocean is a dangerous place, anything worth having is worth taking a risk for.

In 1990, that philosophy was seriously tested.

It was a windy September day, and certainly not a great day for a dive. A cold, stiff wind was blowing out of the north, and underwater visibility was only about twelve feet. But his work as an electrician had kept him from the ocean far too much, and Rod was intent on taking advantage of a rare opportunity to dive for some abalone.

He hauled his nineteen-foot paddleboard into the water at Russian Gulch, just above the Russian River, and started stroking straight into the teeth of the wind. It tugged and pushed and made Rod fight for every inch, but he was determined to have a good time.

He battled the wind for about an hour before he found an area likely to harbor abalone, tied a line to a kelp strand about one hundred yards offshore and dove for the bottom. Before long, Rod really was having a good time, and had filled a bag with abalone.

Rod surfaced and put the bag in the hollowed-out portion of the paddleboard. It was a good haul, but he decided to head down for another batch of treasured mollusks. Rod held onto his board and breathed deeply, preparing for his freedive descent. Suddenly, something smashed Rod, and everything went dark.

A massive great white shark had erupted from the water with jaws agape and engulfed Rod's head so quickly that the lights went out before Rod saw what happened.

Like a bolt of lightning, the shark's lower teeth knocked Rod's mask around his neck while its upper teeth peeled his wet suit hood off his forehead and down to his neck.

Rod wasn't aware of anything but a grinding noise and a punishing impact that made him think he had been rammed by a boat. He was puzzled to feel his body being tossed around vigorously while his head and neck remained still.

Mercifully, Rod couldn't see what was happening. He might have died of fright at the sight of a massive great white shark half out of the water holding a man's head in its mouth and shaking the poor devil's body like a Rottweiler dog tossing a ferret.

When he was slammed into his paddleboard, Rod's head twisted sideways and suddenly there was light. He was horrified to see the ocean three feet below him through a frame of huge triangular teeth. Worse, he could see his blood draining out of the creature's mouth and coloring the water bright red.

He groped with one hand to discover what was pummeling him, but Rod didn't feel the expected curve of a shark's body. His hand felt something flat, like the body of a Buick, and Rod realized that whatever was attacking him must be gigantic. His free hand frantically groped for an eye to gouge, while with the other he battered the big animal with his loaded speargun, which he had clung to throughout the surprise attack.

The predator continued to shake Rod as it swam about seventy feet while he fought for his life. Suddenly, it dropped him. Stunned, Rod frantically swam over to his overturned paddleboard and crawled up on it, gasping with fear and exertion. Blood washed over the board. When he fearfully ran his hands over his head, he was horrified to feel that the predator had ripped apart his whole face. As he probed further, he realized with relief that he was feeling his wet suit hood. But blood was coming from somewhere, and in alarming quantities.

He was certain that the blood would incite the shark to finish his meal, but as he looked around wildly for his nemesis, waves of blood blinded his eyes. He repeatedly washed the blood away, and finally got a glimpse of his assailant as an enormous great white shark angled to the depths and vanished.

Rod was dead set against going in the water again, even to turn his board over. So he righted the board by deftly rolling it between his legs, and then surveyed the battered board and scattered gear. He thought he had lost everything except his old Sea Wing speargun, a durable relic from the sixties. The shark's teeth severed one of the bands, but he could continue to use it.

Rod was quietly pleased to spot his bag of abalone, still in the hollow of the paddleboard. If he survived, at least the day wouldn't be a total disaster. Pausing only to wash the blood from his face, he grabbed his bailer and found his paddles. He kicked furiously to free his board from its kelp anchor, but the line had slipped down the kelp bulb and held fast. He was dead in the water if the shark returned.

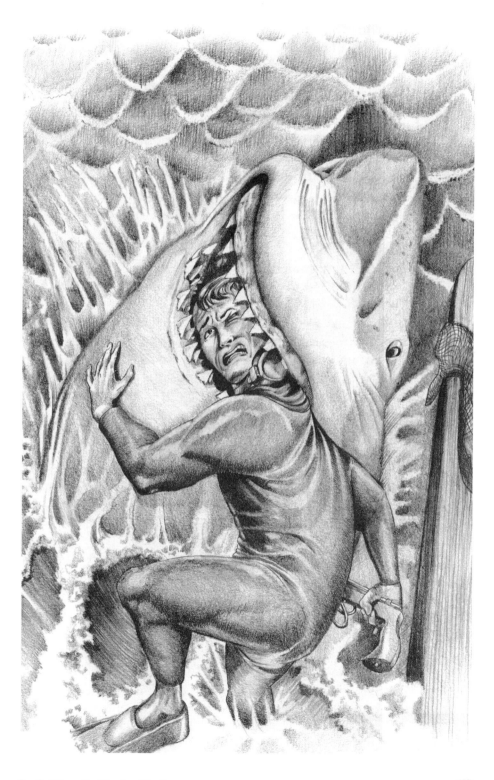

Frantic to flee the area, he kicked harder, but the board was securely tethered. Luckily, he spotted his fillet knife, quickly slashed the line and paddled away from the blood-stained water. The brisk north wind still fought him, but he was so desperate to escape the shark he could have made headway against a hurricane.

Rod timed a wave and stroked over some shallow rocks to throw off the shark, which he feared was right behind him, then rounded a point that cut off the wind. He used the respite to catch his breath and find out just how badly the shark had injured him. His body ached, his injuries were agonizing, his neck had swelled from the bite and was pinching some nerves, and Rod was losing the use of his right arm.

The shark's bottom teeth had bitten through his nose and just below his eye, and Rod thought the eye had been bitten out because he couldn't see anything out of it. The great white's top teeth had punctured his neck, and Rod breathed a prayer of thanks as he felt those wounds. The teeth had penetrated a fraction of an inch from his spine, sparing him paralysis and possible death. One tooth had dug into the frame of his mask, which had protected Rod's jugular vein, and his bunched up hood had acted as a cushion to keep the shark from puncturing more of his neck.

As he examined his wounds, Rod couldn't help but wonder why the shark didn't finish the bite and sever his neck, or why the violent shaking hadn't snapped his neck.

In shock, Rod resumed paddling as his right arm weakened. After a seemingly endless paddle, he made it back to Russian Gulch Beach. Safe at last, he sat up on his paddleboard and yelled to two girls tossing a Frisbee to a dog that a shark had attacked him. They gaped at the bloody apparition.

Still sitting on his paddleboard, Rod waved his arms to attract a California Highway Patrol officer cruising the Pacific Coast Highway. The officer pulled over and a woman who had been on the beach called out that there had been a shark attack. To Rod's dismay, the officer drove off with the woman yelling at him to come back and help. But the officer knew that his radio was useless at that spot and moved to a clear area where he could call for a helicopter.

Eight couples who had been enjoying a day at the beach came running to help Rod out of the water and round up his gear. People react in strange ways to the trauma and shock of a devastating encounter. Rod seemed more concerned about his gear than the fact that he could die without swift medical treatment.

He had one woman fetch the bucket holding his tennis shoes and towels. Rod had no zippers on his wet suit and he didn't want to let some doctor destroy it to get at his injuries, so he had someone fill the bucket with water to pour inside the suit and lubricate it as Rod removed it painfully. As he stripped off the wet suit, some of the women screamed when he got to his shoulders and a gusher of blood spurted out after having been trapped in the suit.

Fortunately, one of the women was studying advanced first-aid and had a carefully stocked first-aid kit with her. She confidently treated the numerous injuries with disinfectants, medicine and bandages and wrapped gauze around Rod's neck and head to stop the bleeding.

Still concerned about losing his gear, Rod had everyone carry his stuff while he hauled his cumbersome paddleboard the quarter mile to the parking lot. He staggered halfway there before the patrolman and three other men intercepted him and carried Rod's board. Rod looked so hideous that the officer told him to sit and wait for the helicopter, but Rod was determined to get his gear safely to his truck.

After Rod changed out of his wet suit and into dry clothes, a couple volunteered to drive his truck home for him. Rod gratefully accepted as he eased aboard for the helicopter ride to the hospital.

The doctor worked long and hard with delicate precision to repair the sensitive areas around his eye and neck. There was no mirror in the hospital for Rod to admire his handiwork, but he could feel that he was pretty torn up.

Rod was consumed with curiosity to find out how badly the attack had disfigured him, so the next day he asked his wife to remove the bandages so he could view the carnage. When she refused, he swore he would take them off himself, so she relented. He looked in the mirror and was appalled. "Oh my God, it's not Rod anymore, it's Frankenstein," he muttered.

During his long recuperation, Rod wondered uneasily whether the attack would leave him crippled with fear. When his wounds finally healed well enough to let him dive again, Rod found he had lost none of his enthusiasm for his ocean adventures.

He did lose his best diving partners, however. Rod and a friend had enjoyed many dives over the years, and when the man got married, his new wife joined them. The week before Rod was attacked, the three of them had gone diving in that same area. When she heard

Rod had been chewed on, she started crying and pitched a fit. "She had been doing really well, and she just up and quit," said Rod. "It made me sad. We used to have a lot of fun with her."

Rod knows how she feels. He paddled back to the exact spot where he was attacked, looked long and hard at the water, but couldn't force himself to go in. Now he avoids the area.

Rod was spared the mental anguish of a Northern California surfer he met who also had been attacked by a great white shark. The night before he was hit, the surfer had seen the movie *Jaws* for the first time. After the attack, he was tormented by nightmares. The shark chased the surfer out of bed during one especially vivid dream. He ran down the hall with the shark right behind him and cut himself badly when he put his arm through a window while warding off the phantom shark.

Rod bears sharks no animosity and even removed a hook from the back of a blue shark during a filming session with a friend because he admires the sharks' effortless grace of motion in the water.

Rod feels tremendous empathy for anyone who has been in the deadly grasp of a shark. He sends Christmas cards to a woman in Carmel who was attacked on her qualifying scuba dive. When the shark devoured her fin and leg up to the calf, she kicked herself free with her other leg and escaped with a souvenir. One of the shark's teeth broke off in her leg, and she had it set into a ring. "It looks kind of neat," Rod says enviously.

Rod is once again convinced he is charmed, because lightning never strikes thrice. But he's not going to tempt fate.

Since the second attack he has seen fewer sharks than ever before. He was appalled to learn firsthand that great whites are the only fish that raise their head out of the water to search for prey. When a great white poked its head out of the water in Bodega Bay to check out seals on a nearby island, Rod's heart froze as the dreaded predator looked at him with its black, lifeless eyes. Rod set a speed record paddling his board to shore. He was going so fast when he hit the beach that the board traveled fifty feet up the sand.

Rod's eye has full vision now, his face looks great, and a casual observer can scarcely see where the teeth tore his flesh. "The doctor did a hell of a job, and my face is so wrinkled that it hides the scars."

More importantly, Rod carries no mental scars. "The ocean is too important to me to let these incidents keep me from it. If the ocean dried up on Wednesday, what would I do on the weekend?

"I know," he says with a laugh. "I'd go down to the ocean and look for all the gear I lost over the years.

"When it's rough and dirty and mean, the ocean is ugly. But when it's pretty and blue and warm, I just love it. I tell my wife, when the ocean is good, I'm gone." ▲

## About the Author

Greg Ambrose fell in love with the ocean on the first day his family moved to Hawai'i when he was nine. As the warm Waikīkī waves washed him up and down the white sandy beach all afternoon and long after the sun had set, he realized that he had found a home in the ocean. His job as ocean reporter for the *Honolulu Star-Bulletin* has allowed him to reveal his love of the sea to thousands of readers on a daily basis. And his intimate relationship with the ocean has resulted in the Bess Press books *Surfer's Guide to Hawaii* and *Memories of Duke: The Legend Comes to Life*, which he co-authored. Despite increasing land-based responsibilities and obligations as a natural consequence of aging, Ambrose still contrives to commune with the ocean daily.